ALL THE DEAD VOICES

Also by Danny Morrison

Novels
West Belfast
On the Back of the Swallow
The Wrong Man

Letters
Then the Walls Came Down

Play
The Wrong Man

The author gratefully acknowledges the financial assistance of the Arts Council of Northern Ireland for a bursary in 2001–2002

First published in 2002 by
Mercier Press
Douglas Village Cork
Tel: (021) 4899 858; Fax: (021) 4899 887
Hume Street Dublin 2
Tel: (01) 661 5299; Fax: (01) 661 8583
E-mail: books@mercierpress.ie
www.mercierpress.ie
Trade enquiries to CMD Distribution
55A Spruce Avenue
Stillorgan Industrial Park
Blackrock County Dublin
Tel: (01) 294 2560; Fax: (01) 294 2565
E-mail: cmd@columba.ie

© Danny Morrison 2002
ISBN 1 85635 394 X
10 9 8 7 6 5 4 3 2 1

A CIP record for this title is available
from the British Library

Extract from *Waiting for Godot* by
Samuel Beckett and 'Home is So Sad'
from *Collected Poems* by Philip Larkin
reproduced by permission of Faber
and Faber. Every effort has been
made to contact other copyright
holders. The publishers would be
grateful to be notified of any omissions
and will be happy to make good any
omissions in future printings.

Cover design by Mercier Design
Cover images (clockwise from top
left): Bob Conklin, Isobel Howes,
Jimmy Quigley, Nora Murphy, Alma
Mahler and Putzi (on right), Gerard
and Cornelius McCrory, Susan and
Danny Morrison, Colum Quigley, Harry
and Jack White, Hannie Schaft.

Printed in Ireland by ColourBooks,
Baldoyle Industrial Estate, Dublin 13

ALL THE DEAD VOICES

DANNY MORRISON

MERCIER PRESS

In memory of
my sister Susan
1957–2001

Contents

ESTRAGON: All the dead voices.
VLADIMIR: They make a noise like wings.
ESTRAGON: Like leaves.
VLADIMIR: Like sand.
ESTRAGON: Like leaves.

[silence]

VLADIMIR: They all speak together.
ESTRAGON: Each one to itself.

[silence]

VLADIMIR: Rather they whisper.
ESTRAGON: They rustle.
VLADIMIR: They murmur.
ESTRAGON: They rustle.

[silence]

VLADIMIR: What do they say?
ESTRAGON: They talk about their lives.

from *Waiting for Godot*   SAMUEL BECKETT

Prologue

Standing at our corner after evening Mass. Girls promenading along the road in the shortest miniskirts in the world. In their wake the faint scent of soap. And a little ache.

An August evening charged with a soft blue haze, nicely cooked by the sunny day. August evenings charged with impending doom. 'Honky Tonk Women' is at Number 1. Neil Armstrong has walked on the Sea of Tranquillity. Mary Jo Kopechne's name surfaces from the bottom of a river. A Derry man called Sammy Devenney recently died of baton wounds and was given a huge funeral.

There has been some trouble in Dungiven.

We head off, Bobby and I, down the Falls to Conway Street to see Joe Doyle, otherwise secretly known as Jericho One, his call sign on pirate radio. His elderly parents invite us into their small two-up, two-down house. Imagine if I could have told them: 'Mr and Mrs Doyle, Joe. In a few nights' time you will flee in your pyjamas, barefoot, down this street and on to the Falls Road, as every house is burnt to the ground, as eight people are shot dead across Belfast. And a unionist newspaper, Joe, will show a photograph of your charred transmitter and say it was proof that the IRA was involved in the trouble.'

They would have rolled around the living room, splitting their sides with laughter. 'Our Joe in the IRA! That's a good one.'

After Joe's we head up the Shankill to see 'Buttons', who lives on Third Street, to see if he has an oscillator valve that I need for my transmitter. Then we walk to the loyalist Tigers Bay, to the home of Johnny Doak, another ham.

I never feel entirely comfortable during these hours in Protestant areas. One night we nervously drank tea in Johnny's while a flute band played tunes from another century outside. Later, his daughter Eleanor arrived home in her Orange band uniform and Johnny seemed embarrassed.

We and our Protestant friends can talk about everything under the sun but politics or religion. Not that I am that articulate, anyway, at sixteen. We operate on the medium waveband after midnight, talking for hours, but in truth there is a communications breakdown. I would love to know what they really think of Ian Paisley (*what if they think he is wonderful?*) or our side's demand for civil rights (*what if they think we are frauds or troublemakers rocking the boat?*). What do they think of the recent outbursts of rioting – which could be nothing, but could be something?

Does Johnny *really* love the Queen?

Johnny's house is as humble as Joe's. He lost an arm in a factory accident many years ago and it is no small achievement for him to have built a transmitter by his own efforts: drilling holes in an aluminium chassis, screwing down valve-holders, painstakingly rolling a tuning coil with copper wire; all that soldering. When we visit on Sunday nights *The Dave Allen Show* is always on the television. This could be a good sign – Johnny's liking a successful Irish man from the Free State – or ominous: Allen, after all, specialises in jokes aimed at the Catholic clergy.

Johnny really means us no offence. I say goodbye to him, not realising that I'll never set eyes on him again.

Standing at our corner.

A moody Wednesday night, falling in love with fifteen-year-old Angela, floating on air, listening to the Beatles as we kiss in a friend's parlour. Walking her home through that summer night's light drizzle, gentlemanly draping her shoulders with my jacket. Gunfire at midnight. Gunfire throughout the next night. Throughout the next thirty years.

Standing behind barricades at our corner, learning to make petrol bombs, suspicious of the new British soldiers. On our side I watch the beginnings of a new IRA, a group that will come to be known as the Provisionals, and that I will grow to defend.

In August 1969, when Johnny hears my transmitter, reincarnated as the 'rebel' station Radio Free Belfast, what does he think of me? Later, I recognise the carrier wave of the loyalist Radio Shankill as coming from Johnny's transmitter, and understand that all is fair in love and war – and both can be very sad affairs.

At our corner, Bobby's mother would be killed coming from bingo in a hit-and-run incident by joyriders representing a lawlessness we could never have envisaged.

From our street corner on the Falls Road on a hot August afternoon, an IRA sniper would take the life of twenty-four-year-old Kingsman Leonard Layfield as he crossed Beechmount Avenue on the last day of his regiment's tour. His ghost and those of all the other friends and foes are still to be seen wandering through the soft blue haze on evenings such as this . . .

THE LAKES

Around teatime the call went out to the exercise yard in Cage Two that the news was coming on. We finished the lap and came in. I had just enough time to recognise the place where I had been a waiter four years earlier, in 1969. I watched the explosion on the black-and-white television, the outer walls of the bar being knocked inwards as if by a supernatural punch, the top floors tumbling to the ground in a gasp of splintered joists, bricks, mortar and a cloud of dust. I wondered about the people with whom I had worked. The reporter stated that the place had been cleared after a warning and that no one was injured.

The public bar had once attracted busmen from Oxford Street depot, dockers, sailors and stragglers, people at the Friday market, some young people hawking stolen record albums. At the turn of the century the lower and upper floors of the block had been a hotel (though I couldn't fathom where the rooms had been) and the old name could still be discerned in moulding on the façade.

I had lost my job as a part-time waiter in the International Hotel when business slackened after Christmas and for the next few weeks had been looking for another job while I finished my studies. I had become used to having my own pocket money and was proud of contributing to the house. Late one afternoon I pushed through an ancient bubbled-glass door which led into a dark and dingy public bar. Most of the clientele were elderly. Serving calls for pints of stout and 'a wee Mundies' was a middle-aged man with a mop of white hair and a cigarette hanging from his mouth. He looked me up and down and must have noticed that I was underage.

'What can I get you?' he asked. I said I was looking for a job – any type of bar work. Some impatient customers at the end of the counter were bawling and he told me to take a seat, he would be with me in a minute. I sat at a table. An old boy next to me pulled a pipe from his mouth and put down the evening newspaper. He squinted. 'Did ya say ya were lookin' for a job?' he asked. I nodded. 'This cunt can't keep anybody. He'll pay ya fuckin' peanuts.'

I shrugged my shoulders. I needed money, mostly for records and electrical parts. I had had only one opportunity of spending a little on a girl, Marian, whom I'd gone out with some months previously. I wanted to have some money for the holidays, though I wasn't planning to go anywhere, but dreamt of falling in love that summer and having a long-term girlfriend at last, whom I would spoil.

I hadn't been too successful at catching girls. I was gauche and hadn't the knack to interest or fascinate them with subtle jokes or gossip. I usually said the first stupid thing that came into my head. Because I had worked weekend nights I missed out on many of the dances where you served your apprentice-ship in social interaction with the opposite sex. I dressed atrociously and was never satisfied with the parting in my hair, which moved from the side to the middle and back to the side again, trailing current fashion by six months. To make matters worse, at sixteen I had a high forehead and looked as if I was going bald.

So Marian was, briefly, my first steady girlfriend. I met her in late summer, 1968, when she came into McGivern's butcher's shop, where I worked during the holidays. My sister, Geraldine, was engaged to Joe, the son of the owner.

Marian and I were both fifteen. Sometimes she was with her mother, sometimes she was on her own and would recite the meat order in gracefully enunciated words that stopped my heart as I ceased whatever I was doing at the back and peeked through a little window cut into the wall which allowed a view of the shop and the till. She was short, with shoulder-length brown hair which she tied back in a ponytail, dark brown eyes and longish eyelashes.

One Saturday morning I was delivering meat to her house and had just propped up my bicycle when I saw her coming out, on her way into town. In her driveway she stopped to talk, then suddenly grabbed the transistor radio I kept in my basket and made off with it. I chased her on foot and caught her. As we struggled in the street with my arms around her waist, she bent over, clutching the radio to her midriff. She began to laugh as I tickled her but refused to let go. I took her steel comb from her handbag and she begged me to give it back. I took out my door key and she asked me what I was doing. I said, 'Wait and see.' I agreed to give her the comb back for my radio. She looked at the comb. I had scratched our first names on it.

I couldn't believe how daring I was next; I have no idea where the words came from. I asked her would she like a spin on the bar of my bike and was overjoyed when she said, 'Sure!' As we cycled down her street like two maniacs, my old woodwork teacher, Mr Devlin, was coming out of his house. He took one look at me, shook his head and smiled.

The following day I did my deliveries quickly, called over, and we went into her parlour. She played the piano and I sat on the stool alongside her. The next day she made us coffee. I asked her would she like to go out for a walk the following night. She answered with a long purr and my heart began sinking until I saw the glint in her eye and realised she was teasing me. I nipped her in the side and she started laughing.

On another morning when I called at around nine she was still wearing her nightdress – white cotton, with little embroidered violets. We were kissing passionately on the sofa when her younger brother or sister interrupted us. Her parents, I think, must have been out working.

Then she and her family went on holidays to County Donegal

– for four days, she said – and I was shattered the whole time and took to biting my nails. A school friend told me to be careful, that she was a flirt and a two-timer. I was gutted. When she returned she showed me photographs of her dancing and enjoying herself in Bundoran and that put me in a bad mood and I think I began avoiding her – the first time I discovered my stubborn streak, a strong trait of mine – to cut off my nose to spite my face. We made up, saw each other a few more times, but then she dated a boy from Lisburn and that was it. And that was the love of my life until the following summer, when I was working in a new bar.

The man with the white hair behind the bar was Frank, the owner. He served a customer, then bekoned me to the counter. He looked at my slight build and asked what bar work I had done. I exaggerated.

'Are you sure you can lift cases and kegs?'

I assured him I could. He said I could start that weekend.

I got paid fifteen shillings a night and when school finished I worked full-time and got seven pounds for a fifty-hour week. Most publicans paid poor wages, working on the assumption that their staff supplemented their pay by stealing cigarettes and fiddling the till. It created a vicious circle. Those who stole resented the honesty of those who didn't, which created 'shop-floor' friction. And those who didn't steal resented being underpaid, were continually subject to temptation, and were frustrated and thus tetchy, despite having a clear conscience. And both sides knew that many bar owners exaggerated spillages (for which they were compensated), adulterated drink and substituted cheap spirits in brand-name bottles.

That spring and early summer my work was upstairs as a barman during the day, when business was slack, and as a waiter at night under the supervision of Roy, the chargehand. On Saturday mornings I vacuum-cleaned the lounge, which we had only superficially tidied the night before, mopped behind the bar, washed and dusted, and stocked the shelves.

Frank's wife, Vera, would appear from nowhere as if to check I wasn't skimming the profits. She always dressed, appropriately I thought, in black: tights or nylons, pleated skirt and a polo-neck sweater, the sleeves of which came to just below her elbows. She wore a small pearl necklace, a style she probably borrowed from Audrey Hepburn, pearl clip earrings and a silver charm bracelet that clattered along the counter. She had pokey breasts and a face that was sometimes too heavily made-up. Vera was determined to go places. But even I, still a kid, could sense that her ambition would be thwarted, that her world was circumscribed by parochial factors and that Frank, a good fifteen years her senior, did not have the charisma, stamina or drive to take her out of the slum.

In the mornings, before opening, she would arrive in the lounge with a large silver tray bearing half a dozen dainty cups and saucers, a jug of cream and two bowls of sugar cubes, which she removed from the tray and arranged along the length of the counter. She handed me a jar of instant coffee which I suspected journeyed daily with her between the bar and her house, somewhere near Saintfield, about ten miles from the city. She had been to Paris the month before and it was there that she probably drank coffee for the first time and was smitten with the idea of bringing it back to the natives. I don't think she knew there was a difference between instant coffee and the real thing, though she repeatedly asked me, in a querulous voice, if I knew how to make coffee and told me to be sure the customers knew that we had real cream. When she left I drank most of the cream, having a sweet tooth in those days, and made up the remainder with milk. I think the idea of the coffee was that we would attract a better class of customer, which was nonsense.

Most of the men who crawled in on those Saturday mornings, bedraggled and unshaven, were escaping from wives and children, or had nipped out of work and were simply looking for a bit of peace and quiet and an infusion of whiskey or gin to slow down the trauma their senses were experiencing. Some callers wondered if by chance we had found their wallets, their car keys, a shoe, or their dentures in the toilet bowl when we were cleaning up.

One Saturday, just after we opened, Vera was up close to me, issuing instructions, and the light odour of her breath reminded me of Marian's when she had opened her front door to my knock, yawning and smiling and beckoning me into the parlour. Vera's breath had a hint of that familiar morningness, which wasn't unpleasant, just hadn't yet been kindled by the day. I can still recall it: it was not unlike the smell of leather after it has worn a bit. I was startled by the resemblance and suddenly yearned for Marian's company – or someone's. Ridiculously, there were times afterwards when, seeking to be reminded of Marian, I deliberately drifted close to Vera and imagined the downy nape of her neck as being Marian's.

I remember the sun streaming through the windows on those Saturday mornings in early summer and humming away as I shone the silver measuring cruets in preparation for the day ahead – naive, preoccupied with trying to please people, lacking in confidence, thinking what album or radio part I would buy with my pocket money, avidly reading about and trying to comprehend the deteriorating political situation, wondering what you had to do to keep a girlfriend.

I wasn't allowed to play a radio but Vera's idea of a convivial atmosphere was very bland piped music. She had tapes of cover-versions of hits from recent years – Vince Hill's 'Edelweiss', Engelbert Humperdinck's 'Please Release Me' – recorded cheaply by session musicians. She put the player on every morning and thought it the Eighth Wonder of the World. She used to sing to these excruciating copies. At the time I thought they brought back fond memories to her: bland fond memories. The sound system played these reels of tape on a perpetual loop and was stored in a broom cupboard next to the entrance to the ladies' toilet. One day, bored by a particular number – I think it was 'Something Stupid', *not* by

Frank and Nancy Sinatra – I tried to fast-forward the recording and the fucking tape jumped the heads and came spurting out like water from a hose. I panicked and just slammed the door shut.

When Vera returned later to check how many coffees we had sold (none) she stopped, listened, looked, then said to me, 'Do you hear anything?' There was a hubbub from a few customers but I knew what she was referring to. I said, 'What do you mean?' She said, 'You can't hear the music. You can't hear the music!' I shook my head in ignorance. She went to the cupboard, opened the door and several hundred feet of magnetic tape lurched out at her like a drunken man. She jumped back and was close to tears. I hadn't expected that. She shouted at me: 'Were you near this machine? Did you touch anything?'

I was a bit afraid of her and denied any involvement. Then I was annoyed at my own reaction: it was only a broken tape and I was certain it could be easily replaced. She had about nine other tapes, all equally tasteless. There were probably a lot of simple plans in her life that had gone awry and this faulty cassette may have been just another reminder of some recurring curse on her luck. Then she got bad-tempered with me and I ceased to feel sorry for her.

She made Frank buy a new machine.

Roy the barman was small and wore glasses. To their cost, some obstreperous customers mistook him for a pushover. When fights started he would leap over the counter, knock heads together and throw customers down the stairs. How no one had their necks broken still amazes me. He came from Coleraine or Limavady but had had some sort of a falling-out with his family, arrived in Belfast and rented a flat over by Queen's University. He was obsessed with his car, rallying and women, in that order. With the women, he was a charmer. I loved working alongside him and looked up to him. He told me that he had worked day and night for a full year to afford his car, a souped-up Mini Cooper.

Several of our customers in the upstairs lounge were weekend prostitutes with clients or on the lookout for clients. Not that I would have had a clue. It was Roy who said to me, 'Did you not know this was a knocking shop?', then laughed at my incredulity. He told me that some of the women were married and were working to pay off heavy debts that they had incurred behind their husbands' backs. At sixteen I could not visualise why such a circumstance would drive anyone, particularly a woman, into the squalor of paid sex, and initially I didn't believe Roy. On the evening that I first started work there, my da and I caught a bus together into the city centre. He was on his way to Telephone House, where he was an operator. I told him the name of the bar and it obviously didn't register as a dubious place to him.

Sometimes on Fridays and Saturdays, when I returned from my break in a nearby café, Frank would tell me to help him in the downstairs bar. The crowd there had usually slackened but the floor was covered with discarded betting dockets, cigarette butts, spilt drink, empty potato-crisp packets and torn-up table-mats, and the tables were dirty and sticky, the ashtrays overflowing. I would clean up before going back upstairs.

Roy resented me working downstairs and said Frank or one of the barmen there should do their own cleaning, that I was employed to work in the lounge under him. 'That bastard deducted a pound from my wages because I was late the other morning getting my car serviced,' he said of Frank, then lifted a packet of cigarettes from those on sale, opened it, took out and lit one and smoked it angrily. Frank himself smoked behind the public bar but didn't allow his staff to smoke in the lounge, though on my return Roy was technically on his break.

We would call last orders at about a quarter to ten and come ten o'clock we barracked the customers with shouts of, 'Time now, please!' and 'Last in the house, ladies and gentlemen, now, please!' No singing was allowed but Roy and I always tolerated a moderately good crooner. Then two policemen would arrive from Musgrave Street barracks. They set everyone on edge, standing in the middle of the floor with their revolvers in their holsters, checking their watches and staring menacingly at those who hadn't finished their drinks. When the last customer had left, Frank came up the stairs from below to tally the takings and told Roy to put up a few drinks for 'the officers'. The sergeant always allowed himself two brandies. Roy set up the drinks but never engaged with the policemen.

At the weekends a chip van used to park at the bottom of High Street, close to several bars in the vicinity, its steamy tendrils luring passers-by, especially the inebriated. After work, Roy and I would have wonderful greasy hotdogs with boiled onions, covered in tomato sauce or mustard. We would stand in the street on those warm nights, the buildings radiating the day's heat, and in his conversation he would treat me as a coeval, even asking my opinion about the political situation, and for a few minutes I couldn't shut up and felt important.

The last bus left Castle Street for West Belfast at about eleven and I wasn't always certain of catching it, so Roy took to offering me a lift home.

One night he asked if I wanted to go to a mad party. He detected my reluctance and said, 'Come on, you'll get a woman!' We collected his car and drove to a house in Dover Street, close to the Shankill Road. Inside, the music was blaring and everyone was drunk or doped or both. A few lamps were lit and there were bodies all over the place – couples kissing and pawing each other, oblivious to the surroundings. Roy offered me a smoke of a joint and I said I didn't smoke. He kept telling everybody I was a virgin and asked a woman to take me upstairs. I was relieved when she told him to stop embarrassing 'the wee lad'.

Here was a door into the world I had fantasised about, yet now baulked at entering. I began to get worried about the late hour and asked Roy how I was going to get home. He said he would take me. I was a bit concerned about his condition but didn't like the idea of walking, especially given the rising tension on the streets.

We got into his car but instead of driving down to the Falls Road he raced up the Shankill Road with the windows open. He was screaming and laughing. I was terrified. I felt we were about to die. He turned at the top of the Shankill and came back down again, ignoring red lights and causing some traffic to brake. Then a car appeared from behind and began to flash us before attempting to overtake us.

'It's the fucking cops!' Roy shouted and stepped on the accelerator. We shot away and created some distance between us, but a few moments later Roy slowed down until the car came right up to our bumper and then accelerated away again. I was begging him to stop but he was enjoying it. He turned into Townsend Street, took a right into Divis Street and drove up the Falls. The road was fairly clear for a Friday night.

'Was that not something!' he said.

'Roy, that was fuckin' dangerous. We could have killed somebody or been killed.'

'Aw, I'd never do that.' He turned into my street, Iveagh Parade. I got out and had just closed the door when a car with blinding headlights came speeding up our street. I couldn't believe it had found us. At the speed it was coming it was going to crash into Roy. Roy slammed his vehicle into reverse, turned on to the Falls Road and sped off, with the other car in pursuit.

I went home, wondering if Roy had been caught and arrested and had given my name to the police, and how long it would take for them to raid our house. In bed I tossed and turned. I went into work the next morning expecting to see squad cars outside the bar. But the bar was shut. Two of the downstairs staff, whom I didn't know that well, were standing about. Then Roy came along in his short sheepskin coat, despite the good weather. He was smirking, hadn't shaved and looked a bit untidy. I asked him what had happened. He said, 'They couldn't catch me.' He said he didn't know if they'd got his number plate, but thought they probably hadn't in the excitement.

A cream Ford Corsair pulled up and a male passenger, Frank's brother, got out. He told us that Frank had been taken to hospital during the night with a suspected heart attack and the bar wouldn't be opening that day. We asked how he was and he said that it was serious but that he would pull through.

And that's how Vera ended up managing the bar. Roy did his utmost to undermine her. He argued with her about the stock, made faces behind her back and occasionally mimicked her voice when she was out. 'Oh dear! I think we need some more Pimms for our *coostomers* from Cherry Valley!' I laughed with him at the start. He would open the door at the bottom of the stairs for her, as if he were a gentleman. It pleased her. Then, later, he would whisper to me, 'I saw up her legs. She's wearing suspenders and stockings today.'

Before Frank's heart attack Vera never worked nights, but now she put in long hours. She became friendlier towards me. Roy and she eventually got on well. On Saturday mornings she would join me behind the counter, ask me about myself, how did I think I had done in my exams, as she made both of us neat sandwiches or crackers, including ones with a thick filling of Philadelphia cheese, which until then I had never tasted. She stopped serving the coffee that nobody wanted. She allowed me to bring in my radio and I caught her singing snatches of the gospel song 'Oh Happy Day', which was then in the charts. I smiled when I heard her making up some of her own words to the Beatles song 'Get Back'. She saw me and I told her that she didn't know the words and that I was going to have to keep the radio on all the time if she were to learn them and she laughed and said, 'Okay.'

She now stood closer to me when she was talking and I

found myself studying her eyes, wisps of her hair, her mouth and the stretch of her throat which bobbed rhythmically as she spoke. She took to wearing low but modest tops and it took considerable willpower to keep my eyes off the flush of freckles which streamed south from the delta of her throat and which darkened spontaneously as we spoke. I saw her in an entirely new light. I saw her beauty and fragility and that her earlier pompousness had been a shield, hiding a basic lack of confidence, even though she was the one who probably wore the trousers in the marriage. On one occasion she actually joined me on my break and I hoped that the waitress would think Vera was my girlfriend.

Frank recovered and came back a few times, mostly taking it easy in the public bar, and coming up to the lounge rarely, as he didn't want to overexert himself.

My Uncle George knew the manager of the White Fort Inn, a pub in Andersonstown, and he telephoned me one day in July to say that they were short of a waiter and that if I got my foot in the door I would probably end up working behind the bar after a few months. The money was better, the bar closer to home, so I told Frank I was leaving. He was a bit dry with me, though Vera wished me the best and slipped me a five-pound note as a present, and Roy said to keep in touch. And that was that until 1973, when I watched the car bomb exploding on television and the old hotel on the corner of the block collapse in rubble.

A middle-aged businessman from South Belfast, charged with forgery, spent a couple of days on our wing in Crumlin Road Jail in October 1978 when I was back inside on remand. Though his offences were not political and normally the IRA would have refused such a person permission to associate with us, I think he was allowed to stay so that his brains could be picked. One morning, as we were being filtered into the yard, he was alongside me as we came up the steps and he asked if he could walk with me.

I had no objection: prisoners feed on the lives of others and need new listeners for their own old stories. We were talking about this and that, schools we had gone to, bars he had drunk in before the Troubles. I told him about all the places I had worked in, and as I mentioned the city-centre bars, he suddenly interrupted me.

'What a small world! You must have worked for my mate Frank!' he said.

'Frank and Vera?'

'That slut,' he said.

'Come on,' I said. 'You don't have to talk like that. She wasn't the worst. I haven't seen her in years. And I heard Frank died. What happened to him?'

'Well, his wife didn't help for a start. She was a slut and good riddance to her. They were married about three or four years when she pissed off to England with one of the barmen and then when he fucked off on her she came back to Belfast looking to see if she could get back with Frank.'

I had heard some of what he was saying.

'The eejit, Frank, was going to take her back. He told me the house was lonely and he missed her, but I told him he was mad. He was very sick at that stage and wasn't thinking straight. You knew he had a bad heart, right? Then he had a massive attack which finished him off.'

'So did she get the pub and the house?'

'The pub was on its way out by then. It was always on lease. He didn't own it.'

'But it was blown up in 1973. Would they have got some compensation?'

''73? Five years ago. No, no. He's more than five years dead . . . He was out of the bar by then. There was no house for her, either. It was repossessed. Frank had no head for business. Full of great ideas and not a bad fella, but he had gone through about four trades and knew nothing about any of them.

'Vera probably got a couple of grand from a policy but she

quickly went through it. She ended up working in the clothes department of the C&A, or one of those shops. She was a right balloon. There'd be a Tupperware party – or something like that – and she'd have to buy everything, even though they needed none of it, not having kids or anything, and Frank never stopped her.'

'So what happened to her?'

'Took an overdose and was found in the bath.'

'She killed herself?'

'Yeah, what did you think I meant? She was on her own over a weekend and wasn't found till the Sunday or Monday.'

'Where did this happen?'

'In her flat off the Ormeau Road.'

I was stunned. A day or two later he was granted bail. I never found out if his case went to trial or if he was convicted.

Four years earlier, shortly after I was released from internment, I had met up with a former internee, Kieran Meehan, for a drink. Kieran's two brothers, Colm and Eamonn (whose nickname was 'the Major' – he had served in the British Army, in Aden, I think) were still interned. Kieran's sister-in-law, Maura Meehan, aged thirty, and her sister, Dorothy Maguire, aged nineteen, had been shot dead by the British army in 1971 for protesting against British army raids in the Falls area. After his release Kieran had got work as a bouncer-cum-security man in various bars around the town and I went out with him for a few drinks one night on the presumption that he knew where was safe. It was on the door of the Trocadero in the Markets that we banged after closing time, looking for more drink. Kieran knew the barman and we were let in.

The place was packed, choking with smoke. The bar was supposed to have closed about a half-hour earlier but the jukebox was still playing songs, most of which reminded Kieran and me of jail and the men we had left behind. We ordered drinks, and on a stool in one corner I saw a face I couldn't quite place, but which looked familiar. I asked Kieran did he know who the woman was, and he said he had seen her once or twice before when he was doing the door. She looked up at me and stared but she didn't appear to know or recognise me. Then I realised she was quite drunk. I wasn't exactly sober myself and it took me a long time to run pictures through my head, including several of Marian, before working out that this person was possibly Vera. I told myself it couldn't be. I couldn't imagine this pub being her scene. I wasn't sure of her politics; I thought she came from a Catholic background, but I had never heard her talk in familiar terms about well-known nationalist or republican areas. I had presumed she was from a suburb of Belfast and was one of those Catholics who had no interest in anything but themselves. I told Kieran that I was going over to talk to her and he winked at me.

'Excuse me,' I said. 'But don't I know you?' She scrutinised me and focused. When she smiled I knew I was right. 'It's Vera, isn't it? I used to work for you and Frank, remember!'

'Danny? Look at you! Danny?'

'Yip, it's me. What are you doing here?' I suddenly remembered that the IRA had destroyed her and Frank's bar and livelihood and felt a bit embarrassed.

'Just drinking,' she said. 'And what about you? Did you finish school? Are you at university?'

'No, I didn't go,' I said, evasively. She looked a bit haggard but still attractive. In fact, she looked not much older than me. 'Who are you with?'

'I was with a friend,' she said. 'But she had to go on.'

I was just about to ask her about Frank and Roy when the air was shattered by a burst of gunfire and people started screaming. Both of us were terrified and Vera grabbed me tightly as we took cover on the floor. The front door burst open and a man who had been leaving just as the shooting began shouted that the shots came from Donegal Pass, a nearby loyalist area. Some men had the presence of mind to jump up on chairs and smash the overhead lights, plunging the place into darkness. Then there were several more cracks of gunfire.

Vera was squeezing my hand very hard. She wasn't hysterical or screaming but she was shaking.

'It's okay, it's okay!' I reassured her as we huddled together, our backs to the bar counter. She was breathing fast and our faces were close in the semi-darkness. We sat still for what seemed like an age but was probably only a minute. People from nearby streets were outside shouting, asking was anyone hurt and enquiring about friends and relatives. A few lights were put on, everyone got up from the floor and someone joked and demanded a free drink from the management.

I helped Vera up and asked her was she okay and she said she would be. 'Look at your trousers,' she said, and dusted them down with her hand.

'Does Frank know you're here?' I asked.

'Frank? Frank's dead.'

'Ah God, I'm sorry to hear that. I didn't know. What happened?' Then, realising that this was neither the time nor the place, I quickly added, 'I'm sorry. I'm sorry.'

She sniffled, near to tears, whether as a consequence of the shooting, the alcohol or grief, I wasn't sure, so I talked quickly. 'Do you want me to try and get a taxi? Are you staying in town? Do you want me to see that you get home okay?'

'I live just up the Ormeau Road,' she said. 'Could you see that I get there?'

'The Ormeau Road? Whereabouts?'

'The Holy Land. Do you know it?'

I knew it vaguely. Those streets in South Belfast named after Cairo, Damascus, Jerusalem and Palestine. I crossed to Kieran. 'I organised that for you,' he joked about the shooting, 'to see if your "bangers" were still okay.' I asked him how I could get Vera home. He said that taxis had been ordered. 'You weren't slow there,' he added, misconstruing the situation, and I didn't care to explain. 'Watch that Ormeau Road. You mightn't be able to get back out. Whereabouts does she live?'

I told him.

'Don't try to come out tonight, I'm telling you. It's dodgy.'

I said I'd sleep on her sofa. A taxi arrived and we left. We had only a short distance to travel but could not have walked safely past the loyalist district in between. She insisted on paying for the taxi – which was fortunate because at her door I realised that I had almost no money. She fumbled for a key, found the lock and we entered the cold darkness.

'My friends are away,' she said. 'I'm at the top.' She threw a switch but nothing happened. 'I forgot. That bulb's gone.' On the first landing she stretched her hand into the bathroom and switched on the light to show us the way, turned, and asked me if I wanted a cup of tea but I said I didn't drink tea. Then she said, as if it had just occurred to her: 'Danny, how are you getting home?' I then realised that she didn't know that I was just out of jail, and that I slept everywhere and anywhere but home, since I was avoiding being arrested and re-interned.

'Could I pitch a tent here for the night? It wouldn't be safe trying to get back to the Falls. And we let that taxi go.'

'I'm sorry. Of course you can stay the night. You can crash down somewhere . . . This is my room up here but you'll have to excuse the mess.'

She opened a door and switched on a light. The sight before us was shocking. She had clearly been burgled during the evening and a robber had tipped the contents of her drawers and wardrobe all over the floor. There were socks, hair-rollers, knickers, bras, shoes, letters, several books, hankies, scarves, lipstick, all scattered willy-nilly over the wooden floorboards.

'Jesus!' I said.

'I know, I know. I told you it was a mess. I've been meaning to tidy up but never got around to it.'

So I said nothing.

'Do you want a drink?'

'Of what?'

'There's a bit of vodka ' – she waved a bottle at me – 'and some lemonade.'

I said I was okay. She poured the remainder into a cup and added the mixer. She switched on an electric fire, but could get just one bar to light, then sat down on a single bed and told me to sit on the one and only armchair in the room.

'I heard you went to jail,' she said, as she crossed her legs.

'Who told you that?'

'I *am* from Belfast. Everybody knows everybody else.'

'I thought you were from Donaghadee or Comber. Some-where out of Belfast.'

'Whatever gave you that idea? I was born at the top of the Ormeau Road and lived in West Belfast until I was thirteen, then moved to East Belfast. Well, weren't you in jail?'

I told her a bit about myself and was trying to work the conversation around to Frank. She sipped her drink and started to shake a little. 'I have to ask you something, Danny. Have you seen or heard anything about Roy?'

'Roy?'

'Roy Conlon.'

I had forgotten his surname. 'Last time I saw Roy he was working with you.'

She burst into tears and I was taken aback for a second or two. I got up, crossed the room to the bed where she was sitting and put my arm around her. 'Easy, easy,' I said, awkwardly. She cried into my shoulder and when she looked up she was beautiful, sad and vulnerable. I wanted to kiss her. She was Marian and she was fifteen. I wanted to make love to her.

'I haven't heard from Roy in ages, Danny. The police couldn't trace him and they think he's dead. But he could be alive, couldn't he?'

'Vera, I haven't a clue what you're talking about.'

So over the next hour she told me her story, parts of which – the earlier parts – she thought I knew, squeezing my hand during the telling to test my denials. She had married Frank in 1967 when she was twenty-three and he 'a handsome thirty-seven'. She didn't know why she married him. I didn't believe her. Perhaps she hadn't faced up to the fact that she was after money and status and comfort.

I had forgotten all about Roy and me visiting Frank in hospital, but when she spoke about it, it came back to me, an image of a side ward and Frank with wires attached to his chest to monitor his condition, as if he were part of a grotesque experiment. She had come in by taxi and left Frank at the same time as we did. Outside it was raining and Roy offered to run her home but dropped me off first. Their affair started shortly afterwards. Had I not noticed the change in her at the time, she asked? I said I had noticed her become more animated and remembered her laughing more. She spoke of Roy in terms I could not quite recognise: 'a brilliant fella', 'the love of my life' . . .

They had been seeing each other for a few months by the time the Troubles broke out – I had already left and started in the White Fort Inn – and then Roy began talking about going to England. She told him she would leave Frank. Vera never elaborated on Roy's reaction to her proposal. (Back then, I could imagine Roy going to England to escape the Troubles *and* Vera, but I must have thought that because I was still prejudiced by my first impressions of her, her bossiness. When I worked with him Roy had mentioned getting out of Belfast, but I couldn't see him wanting any baggage.)

One morning, before opening hours, Frank unexpectedly made his way up to the lounge. 'That's when he caught us,' she said. 'That's when it all came out. At first I thought he was going to have another heart attack, then he called me all the names of the day. Roy pushed him aside and I felt a bit sorry for Frank when he fell back against the counter. Roy walked out and told him he could shove his job. We hadn't really finalised everything, money-wise. Frank told me to explain myself and I said there was nothing to explain, I loved Roy. He said, "That'll last."'

She moved out of her home and in with a friend for a week or two, and stayed with Roy at the weekends. Roy said he had been promised a job, temporarily, but with prospects, as the landlord of a bar in the Lake District. Then Frank's resolve weakened and he began making overtures to her. Roy said she was welcome to come with him but that he would understand if she wanted to try a reconciliation. The way Vera told it, Roy was committed to her but was acting nobly. She followed Roy to Cumbria but it turned out that he was working as a barman. She worked as a waitress in the same place and they lived in a small apartment in a mews at the back, which I thought sounded picturesque. Their life was probably adventurous and exciting for the first few weeks, struggling against the odds. But I am sure that Roy came to resent Vera, her naive enthusiasm, and that their relationship became fairly strained.

Roy had taken his beloved car over to England with him. One day in September or October he drove to London for an interview and stayed overnight. Police were able to verify that the following day he did the interview at a hotel in Islington, after which he telephoned Vera to say that it had gone okay and he was heading back to Cumbria. He was never seen again.

The police had issued appeals and released a description of his car and number plate but there was no response from the public. An appeal was broadcast on radio and television. There was no record of Roy having applied for unemployment benefit or paid taxes or filled in tax returns. When Vera came back to Belfast she contacted his brother. His family hadn't heard from him either.

I didn't know what to make of it.

'It's been over four years now, Danny. And I can't get over him . . . I miss him so much. He was my life,' she said and began sobbing again. 'I went to London and searched for him. I walked the streets for weeks and I thought I saw him a few times but it was just people who looked like him from the back. Something desperate must have happened to him, Danny. He might have lost his memory. He could be in a hospital even now and they mightn't know who he is. I even thought Frank might have had him murdered.'

She gulped her drink and dried her eyes with the side of her hand. 'What do you think?'

'Gee, I don't know what to think. It's incredible.' Given her obsession with Roy, I didn't think it tactful to inquire about Frank – who was definitely dead. She leaned her head against my shoulder and I thought she was dozing.

'Do you want to go asleep now?' I asked.

'What? Oh . . . sorry. Where are you going to sleep? There's the living room downstairs, if you want to sleep on the sofa.'

'It would be freezing. It's warmer here with the fire,' I said. 'I could crash down in the chair with a coat.'

'Will you put out the light, then?'

I bent down slowly to kiss her and she offered me her cheek. 'Thanks for being a good listener,' she said.

I borrowed her coat, switched off the light and pulled the coat over me. I saw her illuminated by the single bar of the electric fire as she unsteadily undressed, her lovely legs, the white of her back to me; heard the sigh of the bed as she got in, and the whisper of the bedspread as she drew it over herself.

'Night night, Danny.'

'Night night, Vera.'

The fire made the air arid but this was preferable to shivering throughout the night on a sofa in an empty room downstairs. I went over in my mind what she had said, though I also worked out that she was only thirty, nine years older than me. I waited for a signal and occasionally my heart thumped with adrenalin when I thought she was about to say something. But soon she was murmuring in her troubled sleep. Eventually I fell asleep, but woke up at the noise of her turning over. I looked at my watch and saw it was half seven.

I got up quietly, eased open the door and left. I never saw her again.

As the years pass, the image of Frank begins to fade and what is left are a few impressions: the man with the mop of white hair behind the bar who gave me a job; the gap in his front teeth; the way he smoked; his joking with the 'peelers', as Roy and I called them. Frank, somewhere in Roselawn Cemetery, his bones sharing a grave with those of his elderly parents.

I can't remember him ever being affectionate towards Vera, though when he talked to travelling sales representatives he always wormed into his conversation a remark about or reference to 'my wife'. He might have imagined that this raised his status and caused him to be viewed in a fresh, more complimentary light, especially if she was already a familiar, slightly sexual presence about the bar. You knew he was proud. He probably liked the idea of having a younger wife. Until Roy spoiled things.

I started out admiring Roy but he went down in my estimation – though not because he ran off with another man's wife. During the course of writing this, and thinking long and hard about him, a phrase he used regarding sex, and which I had entirely forgotten, stunned me and came to represent something of his foul mind. 'If she bleeds, she breeds,' he remarked more than once about girls who passed us in the street.

Roy, the cad, the fly man, living somewhere in England, Ireland, Europe or America, with wife number one or two; the grown-up children; dandling a grandchild on his knee; living under some nom de plume; perhaps with a string of hotels or motels to his name.

Or perhaps not.

A few months ago I had an American visitor to my house, an old friend whom I hadn't seen in over twenty years. He told me a story about his cousin, a businessman from Colorado. In the nineties, this cousin, who had been divorced and remarried, became estranged from his daughter for several years, until one day she telephoned out of the blue, which made her father overjoyed at the prospects of a reconciliation. She lived in Arizona, he in Denver. Then, that Christmas, she suddenly disappeared. Her father and her mother (who had never remarried) put up posters of her in many states, and placed her photograph on an internet site about missing persons.

Two years ago, a man driving through Colorado in the early hours of the morning lost control of his vehicle and it skidded off the road, crashing through some brush and into one of the many lakes that pockmark a particular county in that state. By sheer fluke, someone driving behind him witnessed the disappearance of tail lights some distance ahead, suspected there had been an accident and informed the police. They dragged the lake; the first of two cars they brought to the surface contained the body of the missing girl who, they worked out from Christmas presents in the boot of the car, was on the way to surprise her father and make up.

Vera. I have thought about Vera on many occasions. Her blind love for Roy. Her death by overdose and drowning in a cold bath in that flat, over a long weekend.

Another memory: the afternoon I climbed the stairs to take over from her and found the lounge completely empty of customers. Outside, the skies had darkened. She was standing still and staring at the window, where little firmaments of rain had begun gathering along the glass, reflecting the light of the pale universe of Belfast. Her silhouette was like a tableau from a Vermeer painting. I startled her and she turned and gave a sad smile, of the type one resorts to when offering condolences – speechless yet suggesting the words, 'What can I say?'

Vera. Her silly coffee and cream. Her wardrobe of black. Her Philadelphia cheese. Her trying to sing the words of a Beatles song. Her short period of romance and happiness, predicated, I am convinced, on a delusion.

Her smile.

Her dreams unrealised.

Her breath no longer.

Harry White

One Saturday evening when I was canvassing for Sinn Féin in the general and local elections, I was sent to Plumbridge, to be met by John McGill, a former schoolteacher, whose wife Claire was standing as a candidate for Strabane Council.

It was a bitterly cold but bright evening as we drove over the wild and hilly terrain towards John and Claire's home, not far from the Tyrone and Derry border.

'Did you ever hear of an IRA man called Harry White?' John asked me. 'I was told he was your uncle.'

Harry was indeed my mother's older brother and had been sentenced to death in 1946. Before John could elaborate, I was off, telling him what I knew of Harry's life. My mother's family were proud of him, as was I, which is why in my writings I have referred to him many times.

Harry was born in 1916, joined the IRA at an early age and was imprisoned several times. He took part in the English bombing campaign in 1939–40, returned to Dublin and became a bomb instructor. Brendan Behan was among his first pupils in Killiney Castle, where he trained recruits. When sixteen-year-old Behan went to Liverpool a few months later, he was arrested the day he landed, as he describes on the first page of *Borstal Boy*:

> Friday, in the evening, the landlady shouted up the stairs: 'Oh God, oh Jesus, oh Sacred Heart. Boy, there's two gentlemen to see you.'
>
> I knew by the screeches of her that these gentlemen were not calling to enquire after my health, or to know if I'd had a good trip. I grabbed my suitcase, containing Pot. Chlor,

Sulph Ac, gelignite, detonators, electrical and ignition, and the rest of my Sinn Féin conjuror's outfit, and carried it to the window. Then the gentlemen arrived.

A young one, with a blonde, *Herrenvolk* head and a BBC accent, shouted, 'I say, greb him, the bestud.'

Behan was sentenced to three years in prison in February 1940. That May, Harry returned to take over as Operations Officer in Manchester. However, on 11 July, a bomb he and another young lad were working on went off prematurely in their digs, and they fled. He eventually made it to Glasgow to my great-aunt Susan's, and from there back to Ireland.

Within a month he was arrested in Offaly while giving an explosives lecture to a class of fourteen, and ended up in the Curragh Military Camp, as did Brendan Behan.

After his release from Borstal, Behan had rejoined the IRA in Dublin. On Easter Sunday, following the annual 1916 republican commemoration in Glasnevin Cemetery, he was involved in an incident not far from the graveyard, when he fired twice at Special Branch detectives. On the same day, a hundred miles north, an IRA unit in the Clonard area of Belfast fired shots over the roof of an RUC patrol car, with the intention of drawing the RUC into the area and away from the commemoration in Milltown Cemetery. The police gave chase and an RUC man, Patrick Murphy, was killed. Five young people, including Tom Williams and Joe Cahill, were arrested and charged with capital murder. Tom Williams (pictured below) was hanged a few months later: the others had their convictions commuted to life imprisonment.

Shortly after his shooting incident, Behan was arrested and sentenced to fourteen years, though he was released in a general amnesty in 1946.

On IRA instructions, Harry 'signed out' of the Curragh, bringing with him the details of all major arms dumps which were to be shifted to the border for a Northern campaign. On 9 September 1942 the IRA shot dead Detective Sergeant Dinny O'Brien in Rathfarnham, Dublin. Though Harry had nothing to do with the killing, the authorities included his name among the top suspects, put a price of £5,000 on his head and issued posters:

AN GARDA SIOCHANA

WANTED FOR MURDER

Henry White, alias Anderson.

Born Belfast 1916; plumber; 5 7¾"; slight to medium build; light brown hair; blue eyes; pale, sallow complexion; may be wearing light moustache.

Information may be conveyed to any member of An Garda Siochana.

Any person harbouring this man, can be prosecuted as an accessory.

A month later, having cycled to Cavan from Dundalk, Harry and his comrade, Paddy Dermody, went to the wedding reception of Paddy's sister Jane, who earlier that day had married Mick Tuite. It was around midnight and a fiddler was playing jigs and reels.

They had been there for only about three minutes when the door was flung open and a bunch of detectives with guns burst in. The shooting started and the fiddler took a bullet in the leg while hysterical wedding guests dived for cover. Both Paddy and Harry returned fire, and the detectives retreated. Paddy ran into a side room, followed by Harry, and they slammed the door. An oil lamp beside the window was illuminating them and when Paddy bent down to blow it out, shots were fired through the window. He toppled over the lamp and collapsed onto the floor. Harry, firing his gun, crashed head first through the top of the window. There were gun flashes in the darkness. He fired and simply kept running until he could go no further, then collapsed. He realised he had been shot twice in his right leg. He could hear the detectives close by, searching for him. He lay hidden in a ditch all the following day and night, then crawled to an old shed where he tried in vain to keep warm.

The following morning, while trying to break out of the area, he confronted a soldier of the Irish army, pulled out his gun and told him not to move.

'Are you the man they are looking for?'

'Yes, I am the man. What's happened?'

'One detective was shot dead. Another wounded. And the chap that was along with you [Paddy Dermody] is also dead. You'll never get away. They have cordons out for you. They're everywhere.'

Harry had a fever and couldn't focus properly. The soldier said that he had to go back to his unit; he couldn't wait there. Then he said, 'I can help you. That's if you'll trust me.' The soldier put his arm through Harry's and, supporting him, half-carried him across the fields to a barn. Struggling, he got him up a ladder into the hayloft. 'I'll have to go back now,' he said.

'You'll bring the soldiers, I suppose,' said Harry.

'No, no, I won't. I promise you that. Let me go back and report now and when it gets dark I'll be back.'

The soldier, who was called Reilly, returned that night with milk in a can and some bread. He fed Harry for a few days and cleaned his wounds. 'Can you ride a bike? Things are not too bad now, but you'll have to leave this area.'

Harry told him he couldn't travel.

'That's all right. They know me. If I'm along with you, no one will ask questions.' Reilly brought Harry to his home nearby where his mother made him a big fry. He got washed and cleaned his clothes. Reilly went out and returned with two bikes and they set out on the seventy-mile journey for Dublin. When they got to the house of an ex-prisoner in Cabra, the soldier would not come in, even for a cup of tea, but turned around and, riding one bike with his right hand while guiding the other bike with his left, set off for Cavan. Harry never met Reilly again. I wonder if he ever told anyone this story. I'm sure he must have.

On the night of 29 October, just four weeks later, a double cordon of detectives surrounded a house in Holly Road, Donnycarney, in Dublin. Inside were Harry and Maurice O'Neill, an IRA man from Cahirciveen. Shortly before, they had been informed that the house was unsafe. They were leaving through the back garden when they were called upon to halt. Shooting began. Both men returned fire. Harry ran down a lane but O'Neill retreated to the house. In the back garden, forty-two-year-old Detective George Mordaunt was lying dead. Harry escaped through several houses, then broke through to the Malahide Road where a detective armed with a Thompson machine-gun opened fire on him. Harry returned fire, jumped over a wall into Clontarf Golf Course, crossed it and the railway line and made his way into someone's back garden where he lay in hiding for two days.

Maurice O'Neill was arrested and charged with the murder of Detective Mordaunt. Seven days later, he went on trial before a military tribunal. The trial lasted four days. He was sentenced to death. On 12 November 1942, twenty-five-year-old Maurice O'Neill was shot by firing squad in Mountjoy Jail.

Harry then moved north and was appointed Officer Commanding, Northern Command. In June 1944, after the arrest of Charlie Kerins in Dublin – Kerins was charged with killing Detective Sergeant Dinny O'Brien and executed – Harry became the last free member of GHQ staff.

Joe Cahill recalls that after an inquiry into the escape of Hugh McAteer and three senior IRA men from Crumlin Road Prison, the warders on the wing were withdrawn and replaced by a 'beating squad' who mistreated the prisoners. Word was sent out to the IRA, calling upon them to retaliate against one prison officer in particular. The man who carried out the message was himself a prison officer, a Protestant, who had volunteered his services to the IRA free of charge. At first the IRA had been suspicious and had set several tests for him but he passed them all and they trusted him absolutely. He was never caught.

Shortly afterwards this prison officer called Joe Cahill aside and said, 'You'd better get word to Harry White. Tell him to get the hell out of the bushes!'

'What are you talking about?' asked Joe. The officer explained that when he was coming in to work he had spotted Harry crouching in the bushes with a revolver in his hand, obviously waiting to shoot a member of staff. Joe sent word out and Harry wrote back, 'What did you want me to do? There's nobody else out here to do it.'

The IRA was taking a battering from the authorities, in shoot-outs and arrests, North and South, and Harry had to move away from the city in order to survive. He answered an advertisement in the *Derry Journal*, as prearranged by the IRA, for a job as a handyman in Altaghoney, four miles south of

Claudy, County Derry. Two sisters, republican sympathisers, Brigid and Rose O'Kane, ran a general store-cum-drapery shop in this rural backwater, and were helped by 'a servant man', Mick Brown, who lived with them. It had been a safe house for other republicans who were on the run, including Hugh McAteer, an IRA Chief of Staff who, with three others, had escaped from Crumlin Road Jail in Belfast in January 1943. Harry was now Harry McHugh, with papers showing that he was a discharged merchant seaman, invalided from a torpedoed vessel.

To John McGill I related, of course, just the gist of the above, between getting in and out of his jeep, canvassing voters on farms and the pockets of houses along the way to his house and a warm fire, hunger spreading through me like roots in search of sustenance.

'Well,' said John. 'Why I mentioned this is that the house in Altaghoney, where he was arrested, is less than two miles from here. Would you like to see where the O'Kanes lived?'

'Absolutely!' I replied. I felt excited at seeing the place, which I'd only heard and read about. But first we went to the McGills' to get tanked up with bowls of stew which Claire had made. She had been a secondary-school teacher for over thirty-five years, had continued studying and had just finished her MA on the works of Samuel Beckett, and now, at a youthful sixty, was getting involved in local-government politics.

I told Claire that I hoped to understand Beckett some day. I thought: all that silence, all those heads coming out of the ground, or just a mouth, plays without words, and precise stage directions which you violated at your peril. I asked did she not think he could be a fraud. She said that was possible. All he was saying was that there is nothing you can say. She pointed to Beckett in dialogue with the critic George Duthuit and said, like a true Beckettian, that that summed up her position! 'The expression that there is nothing to express, nothing with which to express, nothing from which to express, no power to express, no desire to express, together with the obligation to express.'

If I thought that, said I, I wouldn't sharpen my lead.

Although the local community was tightly knit, Harry became accepted. My Granda White had always played the fiddle and had encouraged his sons to be interested in music: Jack played the saxophone, Harry could play the sax, banjo, fiddle and accordion, and George and Seamus the accordion also. Harry was playing the banjo one day when he was overheard by the local auctioneer and Orangeman, Harley Boyle, who asked him if he would play in the Orange Hall at Tullintrain. Harry needed the extra money and agreed. He set up his own band, the Magnet, and played in many halls and at house dances in the locality.

The local RUC Sergeant from Claudy, Sergeant Murdock, suggested to Harry that he could get a grant and make a few extra bob by clearing rocks from the farmland, by blasting them. Harry was taken aback and asked him where he would get the material. 'We'll give it to you,' said Murdock. 'Sure, we have plenty of gelignite for that purpose. You know how to use it?'

Harry said he had been trained in its use whilst in the navy. Murdock told him to call at the barracks on the following Tuesday. Rose O'Kane filled in the permit and the next week Harry was given ten sticks of gelignite, detonators and fuse wire. He blasted the rocks with half of the explosives and sent the other half to the IRA in Belfast. Another day when he went to the barracks, he realised he was standing under a wanted poster of himself, which was a good likeness. Murdock said that he had no gelignite so they would have to go to the main arsenal in Derry. So off went the local RUC Sergeant and his IRA chum to collect the explosives.

Harry also started cutting hair and became the local barber, working out of the O'Kanes' kitchen. Customers would just drop in at any time. One day Harry was cleaning his gun when the door opened and in stepped a local RUC man, Constable McFarland. Harry had just time to hide his weapon under a cushion. McFarland had his gun out and was pointing it at Harry. Then he swung it around on one finger, laughed as he replaced it in its holster, and said, 'That's the way we do it in the RUC!'

'Ye frightened the life out of me,' said Harry. McFarland apologised and asked him for a haircut.

After the middle of 1944, with IRA activity having all but ceased, the Dublin government began releasing republican internees. At the end of the Second World War the government also terminated the military tribunal that had dealt with capital offences, and where the only outcome was death or acquittal.

Harry had made infrequent trips to Belfast, usually to deal with communications from the jail. It was after one such trip that Altaghoney, where he had survived for two and a half years, was raided at 8 AM on Sunday 20 October 1946, and he was arrested. When they searched the house they also found twelve handguns, parts of others, and two thousand rounds of ammunition. In charge of the raiding party were a district inspector and Head Constable Carson from Belfast who roared at Constable McFarland, 'Could ye not recognise him, and his picture there on your wall!' Harry was taken to Victoria Barracks in Derry for interrogation. 'If you tell us the name of the line into the Crumlin [jail],' one of the RUC officers said, 'you will not be handed over the border. And you know, if the Free State get you, it will be no flowers, by request.'

He was sent to Crumlin Road Jail and spent three days there before being released. He was then seized by RUC officers at the front gate, bundled into a car, driven to Tyholland on the Monaghan border, and illegally handed over to Free State special branch officers, one of whom identified him and then charged him with the killing of Detective George Mordaunt. One of the branch men said, 'Don't worry, we'll get this over quick and you'll hang, you bastard.'

The military tribunal, which had supposedly been terminated, was now reconstituted. Among Harry's defence team was Sean MacBride, a former IRA chief of staff and son of Maud Gonne and Captain John MacBride, who himself was executed by the British in 1916. The trial lasted eight days, during which the prosecution refused to produce the record book of weapons used and ammunition expended, making it impossible for MacBride to prove that there had been wild shooting that night and that Mordaunt had probably been killed by his own side. Harry was sentenced to death by hanging on 3 January 1947 and was taken to the condemned cell in Mountjoy Prison.

His defence then made an application to the Court of Criminal Appeal, which had the effect of automatically postponing the hanging. Harry was not present in court but MacBride brilliantly refuted the state's case. The appeal was won and the sentence was reduced to twelve years for manslaughter. But Harry's luck didn't stop there. The previous July, Sean MacBride had established a political party, Clann na Poblachta, which won ten seats in February 1948 and joined Fine Gael in a coalition government, ousting de Valera's Fianna Fáil. MacBride became Minister of External Affairs in the new government and, within weeks, ensured the release of the remaining prisoners in Portlaoise Prison, including Harry.

In the early 1950s Harry married Kathleen O'Callaghan from Caherina, Tralee, County Kerry. They had a family and settled in Dublin. When the Troubles broke out in 1969, he began smuggling weapons into the North, and in the IRA split of 1970 he supported the Provisional side of the movement. He was a fundamentalist, a purist who was suspicious of politics. He disagreed with many of the decisions later taken by the republican leadership, especially the increasing emphasis on electoral politics. He died in Dublin in 1989 and was buried in Glasnevin Cemetery in a simple but moving republican ceremony, organised by friends in the National Graves Association. His wife Kathleen died five years later, in August 1994.

Back when I stayed with him in Dublin we used to talk the nights away. I remember the night he told me about his escape from England and about arriving at my great-auntie Susan's house. Uinseann Mac Eoin's book, *Harry*, written in the first person but based on Mac Eoin's interviews with Harry, describes the conversation he had with my Auntie Susan when he and his young comrade suddenly arrived at her door in Glasgow.

> 'Are you going out?' said I.
>
>   'I am going to Lourdes,' she said, 'but I held back because I knew you were coming here. I should have been on the nine o'clock for Dover, but I waited for you. I dreamed about you all last night. It must have been the lucky caul you were born with that saved you. Stay here now for a few days while I go for a later train.'

We were in the sitting room of his home in Shanliss Drive, Santry, where I slept on a bed settee. I had arrived in late – it was well after midnight – and he poured us a drink. However, the version he told me was different from the one that appeared in the book. He said that when Auntie Susan opened the door, and before she let him in, she looked at him for a few moments, then said: 'You've got blood on your hands.'

I remember how at those words the hair stood up on the back of my neck, as if that same electricity he must have felt at hearing them spoken now shot through me. And whenever I think about those words, a shiver runs down my spine, as if their truth were being addressed to me.

ALTAGHONEY

The sisters, Brigid and Rose O'Kane, were arrested at Altaghoney with Harry. Under questioning they insisted upon their innocence and said they didn't know Harry's true identity, just that he had answered an advertisement they had placed in the local paper. They were charged with possession of explosives, and were returned for trial. But after four months the prosecution dropped the case and they were discharged.

As John McGill and I made our approach to Altaghoney, he pointed out the house. I didn't know what to expect, because the roof looked fairly good from a distance, but as we turned off the road it became clear that the house was derelict. A fringe of straggly grasses spilled out of the guttering. Some of the old mortar had fallen from the front wall, exposing the original stonework. And the two walls of the storeroom, to the right of the house, had fallen in completely. To cross the threshold you had to negotiate nettles. The front door had been wrenched from its hinges. All the windows were broken: on the kitchen window a torn curtain with a pattern of fading green petals on a rinsed blue background hung, lifeless, despite a sturdy breeze. Light was falling and we only had a short time for a quick look round, so we decided to come back later and set aside a full morning for a thorough search.

Upon our return, we entered to the right of the hall. The ancient shop counter was still there, as were dreary cupboards on the wall. About the place lay broken cups and plates, black pots, old medicine bottles and capsules, a chimney brush, a single wellington boot, a rusted Singer sewing machine, '7 o'clock' razor blades still folded in their little envelopes, spools, hairbrushes, shoes, hundreds of religious magazines and glass sweetie jars such as you used to see in old-fashioned shops. The shop had doubled as a drapery store and there were samples and half-cut bolts of cloth scattered here and there. A thin slime covered the rotted floorboards. Every time I lifted an object something crawled out from beneath and made me squirm.

So this is where he had lived for over two years, I thought. Over in the kitchen is where he had cut hair and been surprised by the joking Constable McFarland. Over there he had sat and mended broken clocks, entertained folk on his banjo and had been seized in a dawn raid before he could once again draw his gun and scatter a search party with a few shots.

John looked around but couldn't locate the secret hole behind the counter where Harry had planned to hide in the event of a raid.

Across the hall, in the small living room, mildew had colonised the surfaces, and the elements of winter and summer had done their work in the walls. The rooms had obviously been plundered for hidden money and valuables. Some broken crockery and other bits and pieces were lying around. I trod carefully – and not just for a secure foothold. It was as if I was disturbing the dead, though we had received permission from a living in-law to enter and take whatever we wanted.

Throughout the history of humankind, relics of the dead – not just their remains – have often been considered sacred, or of sentimental value, as if a distillation of a soul dwells in or lingers on the touched object, as if the aura of a loved one is preserved in a hairbrush or favourite book they owned.

I searched all around the place and in the drawers of a table, and on top of this table, covered in mouse droppings and the tail feathers of a crow, I found religious literature, little Mass cards, prayer books, photos and letters which I gathered up and put in a box to examine later.

I find the commonplace remarkable – it's what I love about the adventure of my life, being constantly surprised, guessing, answering. In everyday life I regularly misinterpret situations.

Alternative scenarios, often bizarre, suggest themselves. Scenes defamiliarise before my very eyes. A face before me can remind me of another person from my past or someone famous. In the middle of someone talking to me they could trigger an idea and I could have them in bed or dead or rich or poor, or I want to steal some gems from their monologue, and wish they would just run away so that I can record the lyric of my idea before it vanishes.

I am always making connections, many false, but ingenious nonetheless. I would have tilted at *those* windmills. When Ben Jonson or Christopher Marlowe said that in drink he could see the Carthaginians fighting on his big toenail, I knew exactly what he meant, except that I can see things *sober*. That's why I enjoy the world of writing, particularly fiction, with its vast scope for the distillation of meaning from madness.

In this house I found what I was looking for: evidence of my Uncle Harry's enduring friendship with Brigid and Rose and Altaghoney. When I found the connections it felt magic. I was delighted and excited. I came across a photograph, well-preserved, of Harry emerging from a preliminary court hearing at Chancery Place, Dublin, in October 1946, handcuffed to a detective and accompanied by seven armed Branch men. He has just been charged with the murder of Detective George Mordaunt.

There were Christmas cards and a St Patrick's Day card from 'Harry, Kathleen White and family' to Brigid; a letter from Kathleen, dated 7 November 1959; another from Harry to Brigid in December 1985, saying, 'Sorry to hear you're going into hospital but I hope everything will be all right.' At the end he added, 'Many thanks, Bridget, for offering to send me the old book.' I wondered which book he meant.

I opened another biscuit tin. Among the photos there was one I had never seen before of Harry and my Uncle Jack, walking through Dublin city centre on 17 May 1948, just a few months after Harry was released in the general amnesty. A newspaper clipping fell out, along with a little amber-coloured dead spider. The clipping was a photo of Harry and Kathleen on their wedding day in the early 1950s, outside the Church of the Sacred Heart, Donnybrook, Dublin. There were also In Memoriam cards, in good condition, for nineteen-year-old Gerard O'Callaghan, shot dead just outside Belfast on 31 August 1942, and for nineteen-year-old Tom Williams, hanged on 2 September 1942.

I even found two cardboard suitcase tags. How Brigid had hoarded! These read: 'For Miss B. O'Kane – Passenger – c/o Mr Hugh McAteer, Foyle Travel Agency, William Street, Derry, N. Ireland.' McAteer had been recaptured and served a lengthy term in prison. Upon his release he opened up a travel agent's in Derry.

In *Harry* it is mentioned that some rare books in the house had been handed down through the family, and that Brigid and Rose's grandfather, who owned a bonded warehouse, had his home in Clarendon Street, Derry, where he published a Land League paper in the 1880s.

Upstairs, in the largest of three bedrooms, stood a dusty, battered piano with keys smashed and missing; handwritten sheet music; a perilous-looking bed; a commode; suitcases emptied of their contents – dresses, old-fashioned knickers and brassieres; stacks of 78 RPM records, including 'When You and I Were Young, Maggie' by John McCormack, 'Keep Right on to the End of the

Road' by Harry Lauder, 'The Old Plaid Shawl' and 'The Old Folks At Home'. There were books from the nineteenth century, some of them obviously expensive in their day, but beyond repair. Among them were *The Book of the Irish*, published in 1867, the year of the Fenian Rising; one inscribed 'Mr George O'Kane, Foyle Street, Sept 20, 1871'; and an edition of the first three books of the *Cyropaedia of Xenophon* in Greek with English notes, with lots of pencilled marginalia, first purchased in January 1876, with a penny-black stamp and a halfpenny black stamp on the inside cover.

Inside a suitcase John found a pamphlet, *Songs, Ballads and Poems* by Peadar Ó Cearnaig (Peadar Kearney), published in the 1940s. In 1907 Ó Cearnaig wrote 'The Soldier's Song', the music being composed by his comrade Paddy Heeney, though I read somewhere the mistaken claim that what came to be the national anthem had been written by Ó Cearnaig in 1920, when he was interned in Ballykinlar Military Camp. 'The Soldier's Song', first published in 1912 by Bulmer Hobson in his paper *Irish Freedom*, was first published with the music in 1917.

'Look at this!' John called.

He handed me *The Last Conquest of Ireland (Perhaps)* by John Mitchel, Author's Edition, published in Glasgow by Cameron & Ferguson. On the inside cover in Harry's hand was his false name, 'Harry McHugh, c/o Miss O'Kanes, Altahoney [sic], Claudy, Co Derry'. I was excited at the find and later wondered if this was 'the old book' referred to in his letter of 1985.

I phoned up my mother's younger sister, Auntie Kathleen, to tell her about my find. I began by asking her if she remembered the name of the place where Harry was arrested in County Derry. 'Of course I do,' she replied. 'At Altaghoney.' I asked her how she knew the place.

'Sure your mother and me and your Auntie Eileen stayed there many's a time. We used to go some weekends to see Harry and bring messages back to Belfast for the jail.' I was amazed. 'We got the bus to Claudy, then walked the four miles to the house. We had to let on we were called McHugh. In fact, we all went out to a dance one night in the parochial hall and when somebody called "Kathleen McHugh" for a song I sat clapping with everyone else. Then a man came over and said, "That's you! They're calling you for a song!" I had forgotten who I was supposed to be. But I couldn't sing.'

There is a moving poem called 'Home is so Sad' by Philip Larkin which touches on the irrevocable extinction of every family home and which came to me as I looked around at the desuetude, the paper making its way down the walls, the slumped stairs, the lonely rooms of the O'Kanes:

> Home is so sad. It stays as it was left,
> Shaped to the comfort of the last to go
> As if to win them back. Instead, bereft
> of anyone to please, it withers so,
> Having no heart to put aside the theft
>
> And turn again to what it started as,
> A joyous shot at how things ought to be,
> Long fallen wide. You can see how it was:
> Look at the pictures and the cutlery.
> The music in the piano stool. That vase.

I went through all their memorabilia, the little traces of this family's life, from letters, postcards, their photographs, the books they read and the records they listened to. I could only scratch the surface yet I got a sense of their existence.

The O'Kanes were a good, religious family. Mary, the elder sister of Brigid and Rose, joined the Poor Sisters of Nazareth some time in the 1920s. The order was established in England by Cardinal Wiseman after the restoration of the Catholic hierarchy in England in 1850 (a progressive development owed in part to Daniel O'Connell's successful campaign for Catholic

Emancipation). The order's work encompassed 'nursing the sick, caring for the aged, child welfare, the upbringing of orphans and the rescue of the abandoned'.

Mary worked mostly in England. Her order had two homes in Derry and it was to Nazareth Lodge in Bishop Street, as far as I can make out, that three orphaned children, the Browns from Barnes Gap in Donegal, came after their young parents died. Patrick O'Kane 'adopted' Mick Brown when he was a young boy and Mick was twenty-nine when Harry arrived at Altaghoney. I suspect that Mick knew that Harry, who disappeared occasionally to Belfast to meet his IRA contacts, wasn't the invalided seaman he claimed.

The O'Kanes. Left to right: Rose, Mary (Sister Columba) and Brigid

Rose died on 7 March 1958. Her older sibling, Sister Columba Mary O'Kane, was then still in her stride. I don't know what age Mary was when she became a novice with the Poor Sisters of Nazareth. In the ruins, I found her prayer book, *Treasure of the Sanctuary*, containing hundreds of tracts, including one on which she had written, 'From Dear Father on his last visit to Hammersmith, July 1924.' Hammersmith, London, is the Mother House and general headquarters of her order.

I also found a small diary she wrote in pencil, parts of which read not unlike St Thérèse of Lisieux's *The Story of a*

Soul. The entries are fairly spaced out: 1933, 1938, 1939, 1942, 1943, 1944, 1953, 1972. She was clearly a deeply religious woman, of great humility.

Saturday. Sacrifice. Today I shall go *blind* for our darling Lord's sake. I will look on no face but His and see nothing but Him. On waking each morning I will bid my darling Lord, "Good Morning", and clasp His hand, telling Him we shall spend the day together. That He is all mine and I am all His & when night comes I shall always say, "Good Night" before going to sleep and again tell Him how I love Him . . .

I will especially pray for the souls of priests and the forgotten ones who have none to pray for them. Oh! how many are waiting for our help . . . I must think of the sick today, especially at 11 o'clock when the operations are being performed in hospitals . . .

Jesus – what a *fool* I have been up to this. What a silly fool not to have loved Thee and Thee alone – to have wasted my time with creatures and allowed them to occupy my affections. But now my love I love You with every fibre of my heart and promise faithfully to be Thine as Thou art all mine . . .

No amount of intelligent examination or resolutions will ever make me a Saint. Our darling Lord doesn't want my *head*, he wants my heart – my love. He has all the wisdom and knowledge of the Godhead – the great Creator of the Universe. But he does want *my heart* just as it is . . . it is "little things on little wings (of love) lead little souls to heaven.

Retreat. Belfast, 1939 . . . It is not in wearing the habit or in living in a convent that constitutes the end of religious life. It is the entire conformity of our will with God's Will – and this consists in an entire and exact observance of our Holy Rule and Constitutions. This is the only way by which I can become holy . . .

Suppose I were to visit my cell an hour or so after my death and be allowed to look on my body lying there all stiff and rigid in death – those features, those limbs of which I took so much care. Would I not then wish that I had been less careful of what is now about to fall into decay. That I might have mortified those senses a little more and not spared myself in the work given me to do, and taken less ease and comfort than was my habit. Think of what a little more fatigue and a more willing service might have meant for me now . . .

Science has brought much that has been obscure and almost unknown within our grasp. It has even found ways of measuring and touching upon vast expanses. For instance, the exact distances of some of the planets, their size and weight even. But with regard to eternity, science is powerless to measure or determine anything which could bring eternity within our grasp. There are only two words which can be applied to it – "ever" and "never". But my eternity is in my own hands. I can make it a happy one – or I can make it miserable . . .

There are two small entries for 1944 and 1953. But turn over the page from 1953 and it is now 1972. She hasn't made an entry in nineteen years and now the writing is shaky. In 1943 she had been begging for strength to mortify herself, to persevere with the 'cold, hard, dry work of praying before the Tabernacle . . . regardless of feeling, weariness, fatigue or difficulty.' But by 1972, as the changes initiated by Vatican II sink in, she is ready to adapt.

Saturday. I ask myself the question. Who am I? Try to work this out by comparing my present state with what I was first with Religion, and see how I stand regarding my attitudes towards God and see what progress I have made in the Way of Love and advancement in Virtue.

The sacrifice of the Mass [is] now known as the Liberation of God's People – Our Lord had first to Liberate himself from his human nature . . .

Much of the former practices of religious formation are now obsolete. It is better to go out from Our Lord's Table with a smile for everyone. This makes it easier to say "Sorry" when we are hurt, etc. One remark. Father says the Silence is now only kept from 1 o'clock in the morning. He is stressing the fact that we are not made to keep rules only but to be generous in our outlook in kindness to others, helping them in their difficulties etc. Our Lord was not severe in His dealings – remember Magdalene, the good thief – even poor alcoholics are in need of our charity as one example.

Sister Columba Mary O'Kane died on 1 August 1975, at St Joseph's Home, Derry.

Some time in 1984 or early 1985 Brigid and my Uncle Harry posed for Colman Doyle outside Altaghoney. This photograph appears in the book. Mick Brown also posed with them for a photograph. On 9 October 1985, a copy of *Harry*, signed by Uinseann Mac Eoin, was given by MacEoin to Brigid. Later, Brigid fell ill with thrombosis and was taken into hospital before retiring to the Nazareth House in Derry. Before she left home in 1987 she gave her copy of the book to John Gormley, who lent it to his brother Colm, who, in turn, lent it to John McGill, who came to ask me one Saturday afternoon, during a canvass, if I knew Harry White.

Brigid died on 18 March 1989, a few months before Harry. She left no will. Mick Brown, who'd been with the family since he was a young boy, was able to stay on in the house after her death. His sister, Maggie, who had gone to the orphanage in Derry after their parents' death, also worked for the O'Kanes at Altaghoney and was married from the house to a Claudy man, Jim Mullan. Mick Brown died on 19 January 1996, aged seventy-nine, and is buried in Craigbane. Maggie looked after the house up until the time of her death, also at the age of seventy-nine, on 3 February, 2000.

And now Altaghoney has 'Long fallen wide.'

Harry wrote that the O'Kanes were very proud of their descent from Ó Cathain, chieftains of South Derry, whose family seat was Dungiven. He said that Brigid and Rose were 'two ladies . . . They had that soft ladylike speech, and an indefinable carriage which placed them apart'. A neighbour also described Brigid as 'very posh' and proud of her ancestry.

And yet, in Craigbane Churchyard, Brigid and Rose, to my surprise, lie together in an unmarked grave.

ROBERT LYND

Walking home from the library on an unseasonably mild late November afternoon when my friend, the Sinn Féin councillor Tom Hartley, pulls up on his bicycle and says, 'Have you ever heard of a writer called Robert Lynd?'

By coincidence, about six months earlier, I had discovered Lynd in a War on Want shop and bought a copy of *Books and Writers*. I had mentioned Lynd to Jo O'Donoghue, my editor, who then lent me a book of his essays, *Galway of the Races*, which has a fine introduction by Sean McMahon. I told Tom all this.

'Well,' said Tom, 'I've found his grave in the City Cemetery. Would you like to see it?' I said I would love to see it and at the same time do one of Tom's guided tours of the graveyard. We met the following Sunday morning and meandered through the grounds. A dozen men were drinking cider, two of their dogs barking raucously, as we approached. The men recognised us and said hello.

'That'll be us in a few years' time,' I joked to Tom. Just past the drinkers we brushed aside some wild rose bushes still in bloom, and below an Irish yew he pointed out the grave of Private Charles Hughes, killed between the Falls and the Shankill in the riots of 1886.

Cemeteries are places signifying loss, grief, heartache and tragedy, but offering the irony of a sense of peace. Amidst the sorrow you can find evidence of the black humour for which Belfast people are renowned. Inscribed on a headstone: 'Beam me up, Lord', obviously from a *Star Trek* fan, and, 'I told youse I was sick', from someone who wasn't a hypochondriac after all.

The social and political history of Belfast, the sense of civic duty bruited by its captains of industry, nineteenth-century unionism's unique blend of fidelity to its Britishness *and* Irishness, the rise of Orangeism, are written all over the earliest graves. A small stream divides the cemetery, and in the upper acres are buried mainly Catholic dead, with evidence of a different history – that of Belfast nationalists over the past twenty-five years: 'Philomena Hanna, murdered for her faith'; 'Precious memories of our loving daughter Maureen and granddaughter Kirsty-Ann, murdered by joyriders'; 'Finucane, Patrick Joseph, Born 21 March 1949 – killed 12 February 1989. We will love you forever.'

When the City Cemetery was first opened in 1869, the Catholic bishop of Belfast was in dispute with the corporation over the issue of consecrated ground. A compromise was found, involving the building of a wall *below ground* which separates the Protestant and Catholic dead, although the bishop shortly afterwards opened Milltown, just across the Falls Road, as a Catholic cemetery.

The inscriptions on many of the stones in the city cemetery show us unionism's commitment to Britain and its empire: 'He served with honour and distinction in the Crimea'; 'Killed in action at Lindley, South Africa'. 'Write me as one that loves his fellow man', says the inscription over Major George Horner Gaffiken, who died on the first day of the Battle of the Somme in 1916.

Some graves of prominent unionists, if not adorned with the draped urns representing sorrow, are crested with Celtic crosses and their headstones are inscribed in Irish or *cló Gaelach* script. Richard Rutledge Kane's inscription reads, 'Faithful pastor, gifted orator and loyal Irish patriot'. It was he who as Grandmaster of the Belfast Orangemen led the notorious Randolph Churchill onto the stage of the Ulster Hall in 1886, during the anti-Home Rule campaign, when Churchill urged the Orangemen to defy the government. In a letter to his friend, James Fitzgibbon, Lord Chief Justice of Ireland, Churchill had written: 'I decided some time ago that if Gladstone went for Home Rule the Orange Card was the one to play. Please God it may turn out to be the ace of trumps . . . '

Churchill promised to 'agitate Ulster even to resistance beyond constitutional limits'. He ended his seditious speech in the Ulster Hall to thunderous applause with an adaptation of Thomas Campbell's war poem, 'Hohenlinden':

> The combat deepens; on, ye brave,
> Who rush to glory or the grave.
> Wave, Ulster – all thy banners wave,
> And charge with all thy chivalry.

The communal strife he whipped up came to a head that summer, when Catholic navvies in the shipyard had to flee their fellow workers by jumping into the water. One youth, James Curran, drowned; many others were severely beaten. Among the fifty people killed in riots across Belfast were women and children, policemen and soldiers, including Private Charles Hughes and a Head Constable William Gardiner, both killed by two loyalists. A year later, one of the loyalists charged with murdering Gardiner went on trial before Lord Chief Justice Fitzgibbon, Churchill's friend, and was found not guilty by an all-Protestant jury, despite the eyewitness testimony of RIC officers.

Further up the cemetery is the forgotten grave of Sam Thompson, the playwright – 'His was the voice of many men'. A production of Thompson's *Over the Bridge* was cancelled in 1957 because its directors thought it too controversial. The setting was the Harland and Wolff shipyard and the theme was – *déjà vu* – the pogroms against Catholic workers there between 1920 and 1922, and in 1935.

Also buried here are Sir Edward James Harland (died 1896), and Lord William James Pirrie, the shipyard chairman who proposed the concept of the *Titanic* and whose nephew, draughtsman Thomas Andrews, drowned on its ill-fated maiden voyage. It was Andrews who explained to Captain Smith the mathematical certainty that the *Titanic* would sink.

The word went down the line: 'Turn out, you fellows,' the boatswain shouted into the crew's quarters. 'You haven't half an hour to live. That is from Mister Andrews. Keep it to yourselves and let no one know.'

The thought of it – the terror, the panic, the fear, below cold stars on that heartless night – still sends a chill down one's spine.

At the halfway mark in the cemetery, flouting underground walls and the borders of the stream, is a plot called Glenalina where Catholic and Protestant dead are at last united. Lying in a mass grave, they are the one hundred and fifty-four citizens whom no one was able to identify when German bombers killed seven hundred people in Belfast in April and May 1941.

We came to Lynd's grave. Hidden away down a diminishing green alley of trees and bushes, its black marble rises to ten feet.

Robert Lynd was born in North Belfast in 1879. His father, a Presbyterian minister and former Moderator, was an anti-Home Ruler. Robert, though, declared himself a socialist, became a fluent Irish speaker and later a republican, but was opposed to physical force, believing that violence would alienate the unionists, for whom he always maintained a great affection.

He worked in London as a journalist, and while there, got to know Michael Collins. He taught Roger Casement Irish and was one of the most active petitioners for Casement's reprieve from hanging in 1916, visiting him in Brixton Prison.

Lynd was a member of Sinn Féin for a while and also wrote the introduction to James Connolly's book *Labour in Irish History*, which was published in October 1916 after Connolly's death and Casement's execution. About England, in his introduction, he had this to say:

She left Home Rule in a state of suspension, which was apparently meant to enable nationalists to pretend: 'All will be well at the end of the war', and to enable Ulstermen also to pretend (in an entirely opposite sense), 'Yes, all will be well at the end of the war.' Thus, at the outbreak of the war, while England was given a great ideal, Ireland was given only a lie. Thousands of Irishmen, no doubt, insisted on making the great ideal their own, and in dying for it they have consciously laid down their lives for Ireland. But others were unable to see the ideal for the lie, and they too of set purpose laid down their lives for Ireland. To blame Ulster for all this is sheer dishonesty. It is not Ulster, but the British backers of Ulster, who must bear the responsibility for all that has occurred within the last four or five years in Ireland. Ulster would have come to terms with the rest of Ireland long ago if the unionist leaders and the cavalry officers of the Curragh had told her plainly that she could no longer reckon on their support. The Ulster problem is at bottom not an Irish problem but an English problem; and it is for England to settle it.

Lynd was also a great admirer of Lieutenant Tom Kettle, who died at Guinchy, and of Arthur Griffith, the founder of Sinn Féin, about whom he wrote: 'His mind was in one sense narrow: he was capable of bitter injustice to political opponents. At the same time, he had a large-minded conception of nationality and wished to create an Irish civilisation that would be as acceptable ultimately to the old unionists as to the nationalists.'

Lynd, who never lost his Belfast accent, remained in London, writing for the *New Statesman* and the *News Chronicle*. He was described as a tall figure who walked through London with an untidy appearance, his pockets full of newspapers and books. When James Joyce and Nora Barnacle got married in 1931, their wedding lunch was held in Lynd's home. A friend, H. L. Morrow, said about him: 'He had an incessant interest in other people's lives and points of view. I have champed impatiently while he chatted (at utter random it seemed) with a beggar, a waiter, a bus conductor, about tomorrow's race meeting at Kempton Park, the budget or last night's thunderstorm. A week, a month, maybe a year later, it has all come out, out in a "Y.Y." essay [his pseudonym in the *New Statesman* and *Nation*].'

One of Lynd's favourite stories was of a stranger to Belfast who, seeing a crowd gathered after a street accident, asked one of them what had happened. 'Afallafallaffalarri,' he was told. The stranger repeated his question and was given the same answer, which he thought was in Gaelic until someone explained that 'A fella fell off a lorry.'

Lynd published over thirty books and was ranked alongside the essayist Max Beerbohm, yet apart from a rearguard rescue of some of his essays by Sean McMahon and Lilliput Press in 1990, he has been neglected, excluded even from Field Day's monumental *Anthology of Irish Writing*.

Hermann Hesse once remarked to Jung that it was his lifelong principle to review only those books about which he could say something favourable. He wanted to avoid cruelty or destroying the tyro novelist. Some of the views expressed by Lynd reminded me of that sentiment. Lynd, in his essay, 'Tolerant Versus Intolerant Criticism' (1931) wrote:

> . . . we have no right to demand genius of any kind at all. The ordinary book is not planned by its author as immortal literature, and is not published as immortal literature; and to condemn it for not being what it was never meant to be is foolish and off the mark . . . Even in exposing humbug, however, I hold that a critic should remain as tolerant as he possibly can . . .
>
> Intolerance is best, in my opinion, when it is directed against established reputations. A really good writer cannot be injured by hostile criticism except in his susceptibilities . . .
>
> In the history of criticism, I think, however, it will be found that the greatest critics have been appreciators, not

detractors. This may be due partly to the fact that they have written for the most part about the dead. For, in literature, we can know more about the dead than about the living, and the dead whose books have survived have generally some virtue worth praising.'

Lynd drank, loved gambling and smoked one hundred cigarettes a day. He still kept an eye on his native soil. He wrote: 'I never thought of the Ulsterman as the grim dour figure that he is sometimes painted.' Shortly before his death, he wrote to the press condemning the campaign of the Anti-Partition League as 'highly inflammable'.

The APL was established after a meeting in Dungannon on 15 November 1945, called by Stormont MP Eddie McAteer (a brother of Hugh McAteer, the former IRA chief of staff). The Socialist Republican Party and the Ulster Union Club – both of which had had a substantial Protestant membership – who had not been invited, denounced the meeting as a 'sectarian manoeuvre'. The APL represented Catholic small businessmen and professionals: it was clergy-dominated and conservative, and its support was largely rural. Its election candidates were financed by Catholic church-gate collections and by the Southern political parties. In response to the declaration of a republic by the Dublin government and the APL, the Stormont government called a snap election in February 1949 and successfully exploited the fears of Protestants to consolidate its position. During the election there were sectarian clashes and violence from which Lynd recoiled.

Lynd died of emphysema in London at the age of seventy, on 6 October 1949. There were tributes from George Bernard Shaw and Sean O'Casey. Lynd's remains were removed to Melville's Private Mortuary, Townsend Street, Belfast, and he was buried here on the Falls Road at half past eleven on the morning of Monday 10 October. The Union flag at Inst. College, his old school, hung at half-mast. His wife was too ill to attend but a daughter and three surviving sisters were present at the interment. Also present were a remarkable number of dignitaries from different walks of life, showing just how well he was regarded. Among the mourners were his old school friends Air Vice-Marshall Sir William Tyrrell and Sam Porter, then Lord Chief Justice; Lynd's nephew, Robert Lowry, a future Lord Chief Justice (who in 1978 would acquit Gerry Adams of an IRA-membership charge); the artist William Conor; the former IRA chief of staff, Seán MacBride, then Minister of External Affairs of the Dublin government; MacBride's assistant, Conor Cruise O'Brien; and Senator Denis Ireland.

Many years before his death, Lynd wrote: 'I should have felt a sharp pang if it had been foretold that I should be buried anywhere except in my own country, and I was particular even to the exact spot in that . . . It seems as though we must be surer that life is worth living than that death is worth dying. But even on this matter, there is room for hope.'

Robert Lynd was a united Irishman, if ever there was one.

PROTECTED BY THE HAND OF GOD

My mother kept everything: packed old ration books, letters and papers away in suitcases; kept scarves, hats and shoes in the bottom of the wardrobe. She was the keeper of family memories, pasting photographs into albums and stuffing a miscellany of old school-exercise books, her kids' drawings, deep into unfrequented nooks and crannies. Underneath the pillows of the sofa and chairs she kept brown paper and leftover cuts of wallpaper, which she used to back our schoolbooks. She kept hairbrushes, hair-rollers, spools of thread, balls of wool, knitting patterns, playing cards, scapulars, relics and medals – old knick-knacks, which she crammed into drawers or under the stairs. I remember a tin of black dubbin which came with us from 17 Corby Way to 2 Corby Way to 27 Iveagh Parade. No one ever used it. But it was part of our family belongings.

On my bed was a great patchwork quilt that had survived generations until I disgustingly vomited over it, the first time I was truly drunk at the age of sixteen. It was stained black with Guinness and ruby from whiskey. I had been working in the White Fort Inn along with an old bachelor, Billy Convery, and after work one night he asked me to have a drink with him. I knew he was lonely and I felt sorry for him. Billy would 'hit the drink' a couple of times a year and go on the missing list, but the proprietor, Johnny Reid, always held his job open for him.

Just off the Falls Road, we went down steps in the lane that twisted and turned and eventually led into Milltown Cemetery through a hole in a hedge. We sat on the barely illuminated steps, drinking. Because of the Troubles, the pubs closed early, but Billy and I drank until close to midnight. We hardly spoke. Billy had a speech impediment and I hadn't a clue what he was saying, though I could occasionally make out the words 'good' and 'nice'.

Later, we staggered down the Falls together, but close to my home I collapsed in an entry and was on all fours for a few yards before picking myself up. I went into the house, where there was a late-night visitor having tea. My mother gave me a piece of apple tart and a glass of milk, which I finished. I then made my excuses and went to bed. The room was like a spinning top, then the bed became a flying carpet and I was sick. Everything came up. I remember in my stupor joining the four corners of the quilt in the middle, lifting it off the bed and sticking it behind the door until morning. I was surprised my mother didn't hit the roof. She said I must have had a stomach bug, or else the cake was off!

Like her, I'm a bit of a hoarder, though occasionally I am forced to clear stuff out, a job I undertake hesitatingly, uncertainly, and with a twinge of conscience. Inevitably, within a week of throwing some item away I find I desperately need it.

That is life.

I was searching through an old case for a press cutting I thought I had and began unearthing material: embarrassing O-Level results from August 1969, a fading laminated card bearing the Prayer to St Joseph (which was supposed to protect you from imprisonment, especially internment), my internment order from 1972 and photographs I had long forgotten about – proofs of former existences as baby, child, teenager and young man. I felt a mixture of delight, alarm and sadness looking through these old photographs and memory cards of the dead.

Here is one of me leaning over and kissing Mrs Nora Murphy on the cheek as we sat on her doorstep at 5 Sevastopol Street on a sunny summer's afternoon about five weeks before her death. Going through her door was like entering your own mother's house. She was a wonderful, strong woman of unlimited kindness. It was in her parlour that I got my lunch and flirted with her daughter. It was here that I read and transcribed many of the freshly smuggled short stories and poems from Bobby Sands while he was on the blanket protest

.

Nora was born Nora McDermott in 72 Kilburn Street (in the 'Village' area of Belfast). Her father, Thomas, worked as a porter. Their family was driven out by loyalists in the 1930s. In the 1936 Belfast Street Directory, 72 Kilburn Street is simply recorded as 'vacant'. Despite this experience, Nora was never sectarian. She continued to shop on the Shankill Road throughout the Troubles, proclaiming that that was where you got all the bargains.

One Friday afternoon loyalists planted a no-warning car bomb close to an off-licence in Dunlewey Street, next to Sevastopol Street. It was rumoured that they had been attempting to blow up the Sinn Féin offices just across the road, which housed the Republican Press Centre and the offices of *Republican News*, where Tom Hartley and I worked, but that they panicked and parked the car short of their target.

Forty-eight people were injured and nineteen were hospitalised. Many houses were badly damaged in the explosion and workmen arrived to carry out repairs and board up broken windows. Among them was Sammy Llewelyn, a twenty-six-year-old corporation worker from the Shankill who made three deliveries of building materials.

During this year, 1975, the IRA was on ceasefire, but it was a disastrous year for republicans. We badly lost our way. Loyalists stepped up their campaign, partially motivated by the suspicion that the British government had done a deal with the IRA (which was untrue, but which the republican leadership did nothing to discourage us at grassroots from believing. We were told that the loyalists were likely to start a civil war). On ceasefire, republicans had stopped fighting the British army and the RUC but were increasingly drawn into feuding with the Republican Clubs (the Official IRA) and carrying out acts of sectarian violence.

These actions certainly facilitated the British government. Construction of the new H-Blocks was almost complete, the RUC were given powers to interrogate for seven days and licence to beat prisoners, and the courts were preparing to accept uncorroborated 'confession' evidence, which over the next few years would lead to the convictions of thousands of young people, the blanket protest and the hunger strikes. The British defined the conflict as mindless acts of violence organised by godfathers who were lining their own pockets.

On his third delivery to the Falls Road, Sammy Llewelyn was abducted, accused of spying (which was nonsense) and shot eight times. The only thing he was a member of was the congregation of the Shankill Road Mission. He was unmarried and lived at home with his father, a widower. His brother, Kenneth, said: 'He was a very obliging sort – and this cost him his life. He should have finished work at five o'clock but he stayed on to help out after the Falls explosion. We are not bitter about his murder. We only hope those who committed it will think intently on what they have done.' His killing was described as 'The Good Samaritan Murder'.

There was uproar and disgust locally, even among republican supporters. Women of the area took up a collection, placed a notice in the *Irish News* sympathising with the dead man's family and condemning his killing, and bought scores of wreaths. His funeral procession would have taken his cortège down the Shankill, across the town, then up the Falls Road to the City Cemetery, but the RUC advised the family not to come up the Falls as this might give rise to public disorder. (This was highly unlikely: republicans were ashamed at the death of this innocent.) His funeral, on Tuesday 19 August, came up the Donegall Road and turned onto the Falls, a few hundred yards below the City Cemetery gates. Up to a thousand local men, women and children gathered on the road and paid their respects to his father.

Nora Murphy's response to the killing was to refuse to collect for the Prisoners' Dependants' Fund and to ban republicans from using her house for meetings or meals.

I have seen many sympathisers (and activists) recoil at the horror of specific acts of violence – for example, after Belfast's Bloody Friday in July 1972 when nine people died, or after the La Mon bombing in February 1978 which killed twelve people – only to return to supporting the movement after the passage of time or in reaction to subsequent British or loyalist violence.

It took a while for Nora to come around. I remember her explaining later that 'The cause is bigger than the man', referring, of course, not to Sammy Llywelyn but to the man or men who killed him, whom she condemned.

I met Nora's bachelor brother Sonny McDermott long before I knew her. He was middle-aged, very humble and shy, yet he got up and spoke at a hectic public meeting in a local school in late August 1969, during a debate on the defence of our area. A British army officer and a Catholic priest came to persuade us to take down our barricades and allow Broadway, a main thoroughfare, to reopen. Sonny stood up and said he didn't trust the British and that the people should organise their own defence. The meeting was divided. The majority were anxious to trust the priest and the officer. The truth was that many, if not most, of the people, particularly those with jobs, were exhausted from doing barricade duty on shifts throughout the night. I remember being on from four to seven in the early hours, going home for breakfast and then heading out to school. The division at that meeting probably roughly mirrored the subsequent division of support between the SDLP and the republican movement, with many people wanting to bury their heads in the sand rather than face the enormity of the problem – the unpalatable truths about our actual condition – and what it would take to change the situation.

Some years later, Sonny's house in Thames Street was raided and an IRA arms dump was discovered. Sonny skipped bail and went to live in Dundalk, a place he hated. He died there but he always pined for Belfast and it was in Milltown that he was laid to rest. I got to say a few words over his grave. I can still see his stooped frame, head cocked to one side, minding his own business, hands joined together behind his back.

Here is a memory card of Teesie McCullough from the next street to Sonny's. Teesie died of cancer at the age of thirty-six in October 1980. I got to her wake but not her funeral because it coincided with a Sinn Féin Ard Fheis, and in those days, politics took precedence over everything. Guns had been found in Teesie's Braemar Street home in 1972 and John, her husband, served a sentence in Long Kesh.

After his release, John started his own window-cleaning business. Among those he employed were two bruised and black-eyed men whose normal days were spent lying in their own urine at a corner on the Falls Road, with a bottle of Mundies wine in one hand and a plaster cast around the other from a fall. I couldn't believe it. John put these men back together and had them up ladders, cleaning the top windows in the palatial houses over by Malone Road. He said it would get them off the drink. And it did. But after he died I saw one of the fellas back at the same corner, lying in blood, maundering at some ghost dancing before his eyes.

John and Teesie

Teesie and John's home was one of the houses we used as a base to edit *Republican News* when the British government tried to close the paper down in 1977 and 1978, and arrested and imprisoned most of the staff. After Teesie's death, John looked after their four children. Then he collapsed with heart trouble, nature giving him just one warning. I'm not sure if he even managed to give up smoking. He died suddenly of a heart attack in 1982, aged just thirty-five. Without so much as a blink of an eye, Teesie's sister Bridget and her husband Toby, who had a big family of their own, took in the four kids.

Here's a scary picture. Worth a few bob, I would say. Tom Hartley's sixty-second birthday. Okay, his forty-second. Straight out of *Deliverance*, with his three-foot-long, three-foot-wide, bushy beard.

Here's one of me in my First Communion suit in the back garden – or jungle – of our home, 2 Corby Way, in 1960. We mustn't have been able to afford a mower. I just appear out of the grass on two stumps. In the garden backing on to ours, you can vaguely glimpse a child playing on a swing. It comes back to me that a young daughter of that house died of leukaemia the following year. Several streets away a child accidentally hanged himself inside a wardrobe, acting out a scene from a western. Another young boy from our district fell into the Half-Moon Lake and drowned. Another child was killed in roadworks as the M1 neared completion. I didn't know I had these memories. Is everything I did and experienced recorded somewhere and lying dormant?

Here's a photo of my sister Susan and me with the then love of my life, my dog Prince. At school I wrote my first poem about this dog. 'My two-year-old dog is called Prince,' it opened, promisingly. 'He loves me with all his confidence.' At least it rhymed. Of course, the best verse of the poem has been lost to posterity, having fallen through the cracks. It is lying, covered in dust, in the basement of my memory.

The poem finished:

> Last year he fought with a Kerry Blue,
> And was almost killed with bruises too.
> Almost crying I called him with a fearful cry,
> Poor Prince's life depends on I.
> Now he is better and is as good as new,
> And always is ready to race with you.

I stole my father's driving licence. It was one of those licences with a photograph stuck into a small blue book, then rubber-stamped. I'm named after him, so I didn't have to change the name. I removed his photo and pasted in my own. I was aged nineteen: on the licence I was forty-six. It was amazing how stupid soldiers, RUC officers and port police at checkpoints were. If you scrutinise the photo closely you will notice that instead of a Ministry-of-Transport stamp, mine, though partially (and deliberately) obscured, reads 'White Fort Inn Off Sales'. We used our own stamp on the bottles that were sold in the off-licence and paid a refund on the empties.

Here is a photograph of my Granda James Morrison, who was born in 14 Massarene Street. In the 1914 war, he lied about his age to join the Royal Flying Corps (which later became the RAF). In July 1922, his ten-year-old brother William was knocked down and killed by a British army truck in Castle

Street. I don't know what effect this had on him, but a few weeks later, on 13 August 1922, the newly formed RUC and the British army raided Currie Street Hall and arrested him and a dozen others. They were charged with promoting the IRA and fundraising. In court, he said that he had only come out of the Royal Air Force, and therefore could not have been in the Irish Republican Army. The case was discharged.

We learnt about his brother being killed only a few years ago when someone spotted an item in a local newspaper, one of those columns from the archives about what happened 'on this day' in history, and mentioned it to my father in a pub. From late July 1922 to the middle of August 1922 there were no newspapers printed in Belfast because of industrial disputes, though the *Belfast Telegraph* subsequently printed a chronology of events when the press resumed work.

The inquest was held on 31 July. It found that William Morrison was knocked down in Donegall Place by a military ambulance, which at once took the injured boy to the Mater Hospital. Death occurred within a few minutes, from a fractured skull. The driver was exonerated of blame. A verdict of accidental death was returned.

I wanted to find William's grave, and asked the supervisor of Milltown Cemetery, Sean Armstrong, if he would check the register for July 1922. He could find no record of the death. But as I was leaving, he called me back. 'Wait a moment. I've an idea.' He went out to the storeroom at the back and emerged with old files. He placed one on the counter and searched through the book. 'Here it is. I've found it.' William was buried on 29 July. I asked him why it was in this book. He said that this was the book containing the details of suicides and stillborn children who would not normally be buried in consecrated ground, and paupers, whose families could not afford to pay for a grave.

When I told my father, he was indignant and dismissed the story, saying that his grandfather was a tailor and was bound to have been in a position to pay for his son's burial. But it has remained a mystery. We cannot understand why my grandfather didn't tell my father that his own brother had been killed in such tragic circumstances and then buried in a pauper's grave. William never entered into family history.

Sean Armstrong took me to William's grave. He pointed to one of two huge fields with rippling grass, bisected by the road which leads to the republican plot and runs at a right angle off the main cemetery road. Up to eighty thousand souls are buried in the 'poor fields', including those who succumbed during the 'Spanish flu' pandemic which swept Europe between 1918 and 1919. Across the world, more than twenty million people perished in that outbreak.

The grave in which William was interred was opened on 18 July 1922 and closed on 9 August, after it had been filled with eighteen bodies. I don't know how it was covered, or with what, in between burials. Among those with whom William lies are Samuel McKnight, aged seventy-two, and Mary Sweeney, aged sixty-nine, who died in the poorhouse (Belfast Union); Sara Deveraux, aged sixty-four, who died in Purdysburn Asylum; Elizabeth Burns, aged twenty, who died in Abbeyville Convent, Whiteabbey; six stillborn children, gender undeclared, named only after their fathers; eleven-day-old Michael McLaughlin, two-week-old Mary McVarnock and two-month-old Jane Trainor, who died at St Joseph's Baby's Home; four-month-old Joseph Cunningham, four-month-old Eileen Dillon, and one-year-old Catherine McNally.

As it turned out, they were buried in consecrated ground thanks to the foresight of the Catholic bishop of Down and Connor, Bishop Tohill, who said he wished to be buried among the poor. When he died, a grave was created at the corner of the poor field, and, of course, the Catholic Church had to bless the ground in which he lay, thus bringing under Bishop Tohill's aegis all those thousands of unacknowledged, forgotten souls.

Of all deaths, the suffering and death of a child is the hardest to bear and presents the greatest challenge to our belief in God. Walking through Milltown Cemetery on Christmas Eve, coming from the funeral of a seventy-five-year-old man about whom I will speak later, I found a headstone bearing two photographs.

Thirty-six years ago, two days before Christmas, a fire broke out downstairs in the home of Kate and Con McCrory, friends of mine. Their children, eight-year-old Ann-Marie, six-year-old Patricia and three-year-old Dermot were saved. But the couple's nine-year-old, Gerard, and five-year-old, Cornelius, perished in the blaze. The family also lost all their furniture, clothing and other belongings, including their savings. The presents the dead children were set to receive survived, because they were in the home of Mrs Kathleen McAuley, the next-door neighbour. For Gerard there was a bow-and-arrow set and a watch, and for Cornelius a toy rifle and cowboy outfit. The children were buried in Milltown Cemetery on Christmas Day.

Gerard
McCrory

Cornelius
McCrory

Luise
Rückert

Ernst
Rückert

In 1904 Mahler finished composing the song cycle *Kindertotenlieder (Songs on the Death of Children)* based on five poems written in 1834 by Friedrich Rückert, a minor romantic poet. In the winter of 1833–4 Rückert's youngest child, his three-year-old daughter Luise (named after her mother), died of scarlet fever, followed three weeks later by her five-year-old brother Ernst. Rückert poured his grief into about four hundred *Kindertotenlieder*, the bulk of which were published posthumously.

When Mahler's wife Alma heard what her husband was composing, she became angry and shouted, 'For God's sake, you are tempting Providence!' Later, she wrote: 'I can understand setting such frightful words to music if one had no children, or had lost those one had ... I was unable to understand how anyone could sing of the death of children when he had just kissed and hugged his own, hale and hearty, half an hour earlier.'

Three years later, Maria ('Putzi'), their five-year-old daughter, and Mahler's favourite, took seriously ill with scarlet fever and diphtheria. On 12 July 1907, she died.

> In this weather, in this storm,
> I would never have sent the children out;
> Someone took them out,
> I could have no say in it.
>
> In this weather, in this turmoil,
> I would never have let the children go out;
> I would have been afraid they might be hurt,
> Now these are idle thoughts.
>
> In this weather, in this horror,
> I would never have let the children go out,
> I was worried they might die the next day,
> That is now not a thing to worry about.
>
> In this weather, in this storm,
> I would never have sent the children out;
> Someone took them out,
> I could have no say in it.
>
> In this weather, in this turmoil, in this storm,
> They rest as if in their mother's house,
> Not frightened by any storm,
> Protected by the hand of God.

FRIEDRICH RÜCKERT

THE CYCLIST

Driving through County Tyrone on a hot August day, we noticed an unusual number of people about as we entered Sion Mills. I wasn't long out of a Dublin hospital where I had been in isolation for several weeks recovering from hepatitis, and my wife and I with our two boys were heading to Donegal for a break.

There were no cars in front of us, but then we noticed people leaving the footpath to walk along the main road. We were about to stop when a policeman at a junction halted traffic from a side street and waved us on, seemingly mistaking our car for one taking part in the procession. Too late did I realise that we had driven straight into a funeral, that of a former RUC man, Thomas Harpur, who had been shot dead by the IRA in Strabane a few days earlier. I was terrified for myself and my family, terrified of being recognised and of being thought disrespectful. It was an extremely tense ten minutes as we moved slowly through the village, accidentally part of the cortège.

Over the twenty years since that day I have had a regular nightmare that involves my car breaking down in a loyalist area and my being recognised and pursued by a crowd but always narrowly escaping, usually by waking up with a scream and in a sweat.

When we were kids, my mates and I could go almost anywhere: up the Shankill or down through the loyalist 'Village' to get to the Ulster Museum or the Ormeau Park. You just needed to be shrewd enough to pretend to be on your way to your Protestant aunt's or to adopt a Protestant name, in case you were challenged. Protestant families still lived in our area and sometimes the local Stephenson brothers, who went to school in the 'Village', would accompany us as insurance. On Sundays my friend Peter and I explored East Belfast and the countryside out by Holywood, Crawfordsburn and Helen's Bay, along the southern shore of Belfast Lough, on our fathers' bicycles. We had an Ordnance Survey map from the early 1900s which I got from my Granda Morrison and which showed all the old lanes and byways. (I used some of the memories from those cycling trips in my second novel, *On the Back of the Swallow*.)

In my forties, against the background of the ceasefires in the mid-1990s, I harboured the notion of going back to see how much those places had changed in thirty years and whether the lens of youth had exaggerated the distances we had travelled, or the sheerness of the cliffs over which we had shouldered our bicycles. I planned to go to the old haunts, then down the Ards Peninsula to Portaferry, take the boat to Strangford and cycle on through the Mournes, keeping a journal of my journey. I bought a bicycle and trained, sometimes cycling out to Belfast International Airport or around the back roads of the mountains behind West Belfast. But then I got reports that I had been seen in such-and-such a place, and that I ought to be more careful. I changed my plans but decided that I would still like to get away by myself, relying solely on pedal power, and do a lot of thinking. I was at a crux in my life and had to make a decision about devoting myself to writing full-time or going back to the struggle – a choice, in a sense, between the individual and the communal way of life.

One of the central themes in Rousseau's *Confessions* is the tug-of-war between solitude and society, something we all experience to different degrees, and which in Rousseau's case led to an acute paranoiac breakdown. In his last book, *Reveries of the Solitary Walker*, written two years before his death at the age of sixty-six, he wrote:

... if I am to contemplate myself before my decline, I must go back several years to the time when, losing all hope for this life and finding no food left on earth for my soul, I gradually learnt to feed it on its own substance and seek all its nourishment within myself.

This expedient, which I discovered all too late, proved so fertile that it was soon enough to compensate me for everything. The habit of retiring into myself eventually made me immune to the ills that beset me, and almost to the very memory of them.

Many people can contentedly live off their memories or harmlessly enjoy their own society. It is a form of escapism but it is distinct from the introspection of creative writers, who poke through the entrails of their lives and ruthlessly cannibalise their memories and experiences and those of family and friends.

One mid-March, some friends and I spent the weekend in Carlingford. I had brought my bike and did some cycling around the countryside. On Sunday we drove to Fermanagh and they dropped me across the border in Leitrim. I got out at Glenfarn in the middle of a rainstorm with my bike, a tent and a sleeping bag.

The rain was so heavy that within minutes it penetrated my waterproof top and leggings and the panniers containing my change of clothes. My map turned to tissue paper. But I didn't care. The sense of freedom and self-reliance over-whelmed all else.

As Glencar Lake came into view, the clouds thinned and the sun peeped out, and I ate a bar of chocolate to celebrate. A half-hour later I could see Drumcliffe below. Sligo Bay lit up like a stained-glass window. The road from Drumcliffe, where Yeats is purportedly buried, to Ellen's Pub in Ballyconnell, where my friend Dermot Healy picked me up, was pretty tough going. Although I had only cycled about thirty-five miles, it had been against strong winds coming off the Atlantic. But at least I had a bed for the night in Dermot's, a whitewashed cottage situated on a small peninsula at the end of a road which is sometimes cut off by high tides. We sat up talking most of the night and Dermot read some extracts from his book, *The Bend for Home*, which was to be published at the end of that summer. He and his partner Helen were at a funeral the next day and as work was being done to their cottage, I took myself off and returned that night.

The following day it wasn't as showery and I set out for Donegal. Just before Ballyshannon there was a travellers' camp on the far side of the road. A child who had been sitting on the steps of a caravan suddenly disappeared inside. A man emerged, seeming distressed, and waved and called to me. I thought someone had been taken seriously ill but I was also cautious. I slowed down and he came running across the road. There wasn't another person or car in sight. As he got closer he appeared fierce. I shouted out, 'What is it? What do you want?' He had a mop of ginger hair and a huge ginger beard and I became alarmed and began pedalling furiously. He shouted something about cigarettes and money and almost caught the bike by the saddle, except that I was swifter. When I looked back he was standing in the middle of the road cursing. I ran on adrenaline for the next five minutes and when I stopped I was shaking. I felt stupid and a coward and reckoned this was probably the way he menaced passers-by for money or a smoke and I should have just given him something.

I had an awful dinner in Donegal town and wasn't sure whether to pitch the tent or look for a B&B. It was still light so I pushed on and a few miles outside Mountcharles took the mountain road for Glenties. Night dropped like a stage curtain and the first stars appeared. When cycling during the day, the luxury of light and detail and facility to focus had me conscientiously making what seemed like important adjustments to the steering to avoid a minor hole, a twig on the road or the verge. Guided now more by instinct than by the pathetic light of the dynamo-driven lamp, I had no mishaps, trusted in God and was thrilled at recklessly speeding down hills in almost complete darkness. Sometimes I whooped and cheered.

That day I had cycled sixty miles and I arrived in Glenties at ten at night as the bingo crowd was getting out. I asked among the people where I could pitch my tent and was told that if I went to the parochial house I would get permission to camp in a wood above the school. I did that and pitched the tent. Then I went into town for a couple of pints. The bar was empty. They must have known I was coming.

It was a freezing night – there was a ground frost – and I slept only towards dawn. At about eight, sticks and stones rained down on the tent and a crowd of kids in the schoolyard were shouting, 'Get out of there, you knacker!' I sprang up, ran onto the playground and gave them a dressing down for their intolerance. I'm sure they thought I was a madman, sleeping out in such weather. I told them that for all they knew there could have been a child in that tent whom they could have injured. Two of the kids – boys, I noticed – sniggered. I turned on them and told them I was from Belfast and that if they ever came into my area we would welcome them, not attack them. I turned and walked back to the tent and began dismantling it. A few minutes later a couple of kids came up to me and said they were sorry; then their teacher appeared and apologised again.

For breakfast I had two bananas and a pint of milk. The sun came out and I was on my way, listening to the radio through headphones and laughing at a new song which went something along the lines of, '*Aon fhocal, dhá fhocail, tri fhocail eile* . . . and I not knowing no fuckell at all.'

The air was filled with the smell of turf, the skies were blue, I was free and healthy: I was inside my own soul. I arrived in Dungloe, locked my bike and wandered the main street. I called into a store owned by a man with whose brother I had been in jail, but he was not there that day. I treated myself to a big meal and a few glasses of wine.

A friend, Pam Brighton, director of Dubblejoint Theatre Company, who lives in Belfast, owned a bungalow a few miles outside Dungloe and told me I could collect the key for it from next door. I went out to the house, got the key and spent a lonely night. I rose very early the next morning, had some toast and milk and set off for Letterkenny, thirty Donegal miles away. There was a biting wind and flurries of snow as I made my way around Errigal Mountain. My hands were numb, even through I was wearing strong gloves. The road from Kilmacrennan to Letterkenny was a back-breaker, long and steep and never-ending. When I arrived in Letterkenny I decided that I was mad: it was still winter, I was beginning to feel miserable and I was very, very tired and wet. I went to the bus station and asked if I could put my bike in the luggage hold to get to Derry. There was no problem.

In Derry I thought about staying the night in someone's house and trying to complete the return journey to Belfast, seventy miles, in one go the following day. But when I heard that there was one more train to Belfast that night, leaving within a half-hour, I decided to go home. I phoned my sons and told them to expect me in about two hours, quickly ate an awful hamburger, then flew over Craigavon Bridge to the station on the Waterside. I put my bike in the freight compartment and sat down in the adjacent carriage. I had a few days' growth on my face and was wearing a woolly hat. I put on my Walkman to listen to some music, spread myself across the seat, felt a modest glow of accomplishment and began to doze.

As it turned out the train was not an express but was destined to stop at all of the stations along the way. It pulled up at Castlerock, scene of the sectarian killings of four nationalists as they arrived for work in their van, three years earlier. I watched as a number of men on the platform climbed into the freight compartment and passed in golf bags. Then the door into our compartment opened and in came the five of them, carrying – which I hadn't noticed earlier – plastic bags full of cans of beer. One of them had what looked like a loyalist tattoo on his arm. They couldn't get sitting beside me – I was pretending to be asleep – but one burly fella ripped the seat opposite me out of its fittings. They proceeded to sit just across the aisle and use the seat as a card table. I buried my chin deep into my shoulder, away from them.

'Hey boy!' one of them shouted over. 'What are you listening to?'

I realised that they were drunk. I had overheard that they were from Lisburn.

'How many fuckin' cards do you want?'

'Give us two fuckin' aces, okay!'

'I know your man from somewhere.' Then it was back to the game. Every few minutes one would say, 'I definitely know him. Billy, who does he remind you of?'

The sweat was trickling down my neck and I knew I was in for a severe beating or worse if they realised who I was. This went on for about twenty minutes. At one point while they were arguing over the poker I rose quickly, as if just realising it was my stop, and went into the freight compartment.

'What do you think you're doing! You can't stay here,' said the conductor. 'It's against regulations.' I told him that the men next door were drunk and bothering me.

'Well, there's plenty more seats down the carriage. Go down there,' he told me. But I knew if they saw me face-on they would probably recognise me. Nor could I confide in the conductor about my true concern as his loyalty was unlikely to lie with me, and, besides, he was only one man. I asked where we were. He said Cullybackey. I asked him what the next station was and he said Ballymena. I told him I would get off there.

'But there's no more trains back to Belfast tonight,' he said. I told him I didn't care.

I got off in Ballymena. I was starving, tired and frightened. Antrim was eleven miles away. Refuge in a friend's house. The night was now black. It was cold and drizzling and there seemed to be a thousand cars recklessly roaring past me. After about an hour I made it to Antrim but was confused and couldn't find my friend's house. I was afraid to ask in case I was in a loyalist area and, again, someone might recognise me. I couldn't even try a phone box, or go into a shop for a drink and some food. I realised that I would have to cycle to Belfast, nineteen miles away, along back roads. I came through the loyalist Ballycraigy estate to get onto the seven-mile straight.

I was now so dehydrated that out in the countryside I lay down on the road and gulped rainwater from a puddle. I noticed glistening cow dung just a few feet away, but didn't care.

I shivered as I rode past the ghostly spot, marked by a cross, where two Protestant brothers, Malcolm and Peter Orr, were killed by loyalists in the early days of the Troubles because they had befriended Catholics. I found a small stream, climbed down an embankment and drank about two pints of fresh water out of my cupped hands. There was a long hill before me, the top of which was shrouded in mist. I was too tired to cycle up it so I pushed my bike for about fifteen minutes. Dogs barked and howled as I passed a few isolated houses.

At a quarter to one in the morning, having been on the road for over sixteen hours, I turned onto the Tornaroy Road at the back of Black Mountain and with relief saw the lights of the city glinting below. It was all downhill now, and when I arrived home I discovered that while I was in Ballymena, the UVF had burst into a pub and shot dead one of their members, Thomas Sheppard, as a suspected informer. My sons had heard about the shooting and had been very worried when I hadn't arrived as expected.

Regrettably, but understandably, there are hundreds of places in this, my own country, where I, and others with thumbs in the conflict, will never be safe, where we will never be able to visit, despite ceasefires, power-sharing or our support for peace.

Except, perhaps, in old dreams of youth. And nightmares.

AMSTERDAM

Sitting outside Smits Koffiehuis, at a table on the canal bank, sipping a beer, as the barges go by and the sun goes down. Listening to many languages. Observing swaggering young fellas and lads with locks shaved to a point. Beautiful young women whom you could write stories about. Romantic couples; timid old folk; people with small faces or big, interesting noses. People wearing clothes that don't fit or suit their demeanour. All sifted through one's prejudices, opinions, norms.

Flags of every nation flutter from a nearby hotel. Tram bells clang at swarming pedestrians and canny cyclists, many of whom have friends on their crossbars, gabble away, oblivious to their surroundings. From the bridge that leads to Central Station waft the warm notes of a busker's saxophone. At the next table a man puffs on a small cigar and I catch a thread of the pleasant smoke that always for me suggests a state of smugness.

Out of sight, a thousand miles from here, in Afghanistan, in the name of a Christian God, missiles are crushing human lives to dust in response to the terrorist bombings in Washington and at the World Trade Centre in New York. If you hesitate, if you demur in your support for the Allied bombing, if you attempt to understand or try to articulate the factors that may have led to the first horrific attacks, you risk being branded a terrorist or an apologist for terrorism. There is no third way: you are either with us and one of us, or against us and one of them, a simplification and polarisation that I feel has to be resisted.

Amsterdam has a hedonistic image, largely because of the legalisation of soft drugs and prostitution. It is, in fact, a very tolerant city. One brochure reads: 'The police of the red-light district welcome you.' On drugs it says, 'Be careful mixing alcohol and soft drugs.' On urinating in public: 'Dirty habit, always committed by *men* . . . Use one of the public toilets. You can also go to a police station.' On prostitution: 'If you visit one of the women, we would like to remind you, they are not always women.'

We have visited the Rijksmuseum, the Anne Frank House, the Jewish Historical Museum, the Sex Museum, the Torture Museum, the Dutch Resistance Museum, Rembrandt's house, and Ons' Lieve Heer op Solder (Our Lord in the Attic), where, after the Reformation, Amsterdam Catholics could practise their faith only in private. We did the canal tour and walked for many hours each day, building up great appetites for each night's exotic meal.

Studying the paintings, the artefacts, the maps showing the expansion of the Dutch East India Company, I have been struck by the prevalence and consistency of cruelty, brutality, war and dispossession throughout history. In the Torture Museum the instruments used, especially during the Catholic Inquisition, explain themselves: the skull cracker, the grill, the rack, the saw (used to slice people in two, beginning at the genitals). Women found guilty of adultery were buried alive. Hanging cages in which victims were left to starve to death were used by Christians, mostly against innocent Jews picked at random.

In the Rijksmuseum there is a 1661 painting by Ferdinand Bol on the theme of exemplary behaviour. Consul Titus Manlius Torquatus had instructed that none of his officers should engage the foe. His own son broke the order before the battle of Romans and Latins at the foot of Vesuvius (340 BC) and although he returned victorious from the duel, his father ordered that he be beheaded. The father sits on the throne looking away, contemplative, as the axe-man shows the severed head of his son to a centurion.

The secret annexe where Anne Frank's father, her sister and mother and four friends stayed in hiding for over two years, before they were betrayed, is open to the public. In her diary in 1942 Anne wrote: 'Jews must wear a yellow star, Jews must hand in their bicycles, Jews are banned from trams and are forbidden to drive. Jews must be indoors by eight o'clock . . . ' On 4 August 1944, when the Allies were nearing the Dutch border, the family were found and arrested. Mrs Frank died in Auschwitz. Anne and her sister died of typhus in Bergen-Belsen in 1945. In *The Diary of Anne Frank* the fifteen-year-old wrote that she wanted to live on after her death. Nelson Mandela said that *The Diary* had been an inspiration to the prisoners on Robben Island.

At the start of the war, the Netherlands had declared itself neutral, but in May 1940 it was overrun by Germany and surrendered after four days. France surrendered a month later. Many Dutch believed they should reconcile themselves to the new situation. In effect, this allowed the Nazis to control the country with a small occupying force and with the help of their collaborators in the Dutch Nazi Party, the NSB.

The Dutch Resistance Museum acknowledges that collab-oration was fairly widespread but does its best to emphasise the opposition to the occupation: for example, the general strike against the persecution of the Jews which led to protestors being mown down, and the refusal of 86 per cent of students to sign a loyalty declaration to Germany. However, when radio sets were banned, 80 per cent of all sets were handed in, though people built crystal sets to listen to Radio Orange, which operated from London, broadcasting speeches from Queen Wilhelmina, who had fled to England at the beginning of the war. Forced labour was ordered in May 1943 and 500,000 Dutchmen went to work in Germany. But others went into hiding, bringing the total to almost 300,000, made up of Jews, students, communists, and former soldiers, who provided the backbone to the resistance movement. They organised strikes and sabotage, published over 150 illegal newspapers, helped Allied pilots who had been shot down, and eventually, under the LKP (national organisation of armed squads) launched military attacks and set fire to registry offices.

There is the story of Hannie Schaft, whom the Germans knew as *'het meisje met het rode haar'* (or in German, *Das rothaarige Mädel*) – the girl with the red hair. Hannie (real name Jannetje Johanna Schaft), a student from Haarlem, was studying law at Amsterdam and joined the Council of Resistance, the RVV, shortly after the occupation. She dyed her hair black and wore spectacles made of clear glass.

The RVV ordered her and another member of the group to kill an officer of the German secret police, the SD. When Hannie fired her gun at the target she heard a click and nothing happened. The 'SD officer' introduced himself as Frans van der Wiel, the commandant of the resistance group. It had been a test. Hannie and two comrades, two young sisters, assassinated German secret police and Dutch collaborators. In order to pluck up the courage to carry out the killings the girls had to scream at each other how evil the informer was.

It was said that before going out on operations Hannie powdered her face because she wanted to die looking pretty. On 21 March 1945, Hannie was arrested carrying a pistol in her bag. Despite her disguise the Germans soon realised that it was the girl with the red hair they had captured. She was interrogated until she admitted killing a traitor called van Langendijk and was sentenced to death. On 17 April 1945, just two weeks before the liberation of Holland, she was taken from her cell in Amsterdam, brought to Overveen and shot dead. Her body was taken to the sand dunes around Bloemendaal, where 374 other resistance fighters were executed, and buried in a shallow grave. Her father searched for her after the liberation and located her remains when he saw her red hair blowing above the sand.

German propaganda depicted the resistance as 'criminals'. Of 20,000 suspected resistance fighters, 2,000 were executed. Prisoners were not allowed pencils or pens, yet managed to smuggle small letters from jail, written on cigarette papers, not unlike the H-Block 'comms' (communications). On 5 May 1945, German forces in Holland surrendered. One hundred and twenty thousand Dutch collaborators were imprisoned and 34 executed, including the leader of the NSB. Of 140,000 Jews in Holland at the start of the war, 78 per cent had been murdered, often by being fooled into thinking that they were being sent to Germany to work in factories, rather than to their deaths in concentration camps.

There are interviews with survivors and testimony of some good in this world of evil. On Christmas Eve, 1941, a member of the Dutch SS came to the door of the Levy family home in Varsseveld, in the Achtehock. He turned out to be a school friend of their son Johnny and he warned them, 'Never go to work in Germany. There are camps there where the Jews are being murdered.' They escaped.

Twenty-two-year old Earl Van Slyke from Durham, Ontario, a gunner in an anti-aircraft unit, was among the first Allied soldiers to enter Amsterdam after the German surrender. 'You couldn't see the rooftops of buildings, for people cheering and clapping. The streets were thronged. So many people were climbing up on the trucks and jeeps that it was almost impossible to drive through the city.'

He, along with his five brothers, two of whom joined the Canadian Air Force, had enlisted in the early 1940s, though they were never to serve beside each other in the war.

While on leave, Van and his buddies spent their afternoons in Amsterdam in his favourite place, Heck's Restaurant in Rembrandtplein. Upstairs, a small orchestra serenaded the diners. Afterwards, these off-duty soldiers would sit for hours at tables outside, enjoying the evening sun and relishing their spared lives. Van's daughter – my wife, Leslie – and I had heard him talk a lot about Heck's. We searched the square, asked around and discovered that, not surprisingly, Heck's had changed proprietors – who knows how many times – and was now the Ritz. So, we sat at a table outside the Ritz, ordered some wine and toasted her father and his comrades.

I asked Leslie how she felt, because I was thinking about my own eerie feelings as I stepped among the ghosts of Altaghoney, where my uncle Harry had lived, a few months earlier. She said she had seen many photographs of her father during the war, but that being here (this was her first time on the European continent) had somehow made it real, brought it to life, made her feel close to him. 'I'm also thinking of how he must have felt back then . . . a young guy from a big family, from a small Ontario town, having had a tough time growing up at the time of the depression . . . I'm sure the army was a big adventure back then – or at least, that's what they thought it was going to be.'

Before enlisting, Van had worked in two munitions factories. He joined up, he told me, 'for adventure and to do my bit', and was trained at Halifax, Nova Scotia, before being sent to England and from there to North Africa. His convoy was attacked by the Luftwaffe as they passed through the Straits of Gibraltar. Four ships were hit and sank. It was a frightening experience. 'The boat was shaking and rocking and we were trapped in the hold as the bulkheads were shut during the raid,' he said.

After North Africa he saw action at the southern Italian port of Ortona with the First Canadian anti-aircraft. This was a month-long, bitter and protracted fight to clear the German defences between the Moro and Riccio rivers.

Conditions mirrored the Somme and Passchendaele, with attrition replacing manoeuvre and both sides suffering heavy losses. After Ortona he took part in the advance on Rome alongside the Fifth American Army, before being transferred to an artillery unit, learning to fire a 4.5 artillery gun in the middle of the action.

Six thousand Canadians lost their lives in the Italian campaign.

From Italy, Van was shipped to southern France. The Canadians hauled their guns through France and Belgium and fought their way into Holland. He was on the front line at Arnhem. Throughout the war he was separated from and heard little about his brothers. Incredibly, all six Van Slykes survived the war unscathed.

In the Dutch Resistance Museum I read in great detail the sad story of Johnny en Jones. On headphones I listened to several crackly recordings of their songs. Their music was still playing in my mind, and my mind playing with time, as we later walked through the streets of Amsterdam towards Centraal Station.

Nol van Wesel and Max Kannewasser were Jewish friends who formed a famous cabaret duet under the stage name Johnny en Jones in the 1930s. They and their wives were arrested and placed in the Westerbork transit camp, from where the two men during the summer of 1944 were initially detailed to do outside work, retrieving scrap metal from Allied planes that had been shot down. Friends advised them to take this opportunity to go into hiding but they refused to leave their wives behind. They were eventually transported to Bergen-Belsen. There, on 20 March 1945, overcome by the hardships he had suffered, Max died. On 15 April, the day the camp was liberated by the Allies, Nol died. In the 1980s, all their recordings were reissued.

Their music has never died. It captures the unique spirit of another time and place, when, despite the ominous signs, there was still a little joy in life, and much innocence. Hindsight provokes in one a hopeless longing to stop the clock right then and there, while the audience was still laughing and cheering and drinking.

Sitting outside Smits Koffiehuis, at a table on the canal bank, sipping a beer, thinking about these things, as the sun goes down . . .

OLD FRIENDS

Billy McCulloch comes to our house for his Sunday dinner, and some nights he and I sit in his living room and drink and talk about poetry, which he loves, or he'll recall certain historical events which impressed him, such as the race for the South Pole, or life in Belfast during the Blitz, or about all the people he knew in his life. Scattered on the table before him are poetry books that he is reading and letters he is writing, and we have to make room for the glasses and the gin. Often he mentions an old friend, Gibbie, about whom I have heard so much that I feel we are acquainted. Billy is eighty-nine and had to give up driving some years ago. He lost his balance and became shaky on his legs, had to use first a stick and now, this past year, a frame.

I don't own a car but my son, Kevin, who was holidaying in Mexico for a fortnight, had left me his. Then, over a few gins late one night, we planned that in Kevin's car to Gibbie's, to Cumbria, England, we would go! On a sunny May morning Billy and I packed our cases like excited kids and drove on to the Stranraer ferry.

Billy was born a Protestant in East Belfast in the year that the *Titanic* was launched, 1911. He describes his nationality as left-wing or *sans frontières*. His father, John William, came to Belfast from Birkenhead as an iron-moulder during the engineering boom in the 1880s, bringing with him his new wife, Mary Francis (whom he addressed as 'Polly') from Conah's Quay, Wales. She had worked as a domestic servant. At first they lived in a single room but later managed to move into a new house on working-class

Rosebery Road, where most of the men worked in the nearby shipyard.

Rosebery Road, built in the 1890s, was named after Archibald Philip Primrose, who became the 5th Earl of Rosebery after the death of his grandfather in 1868 and British prime minister when Gladstone resigned in 1894. He caused mayhem when he made his first speech as premier and said that Home Rule for Ireland could only come about when England, 'the predominant member of the three Kingdoms', agreed to it. Primrose had left Oxford after he came into conflict with the university authorities over his ownership of a racehorse. Despite not having a degree, he was considered to be a distinguished young intellectual. He declared that he had only three ambitions: to marry an heiress, to win the Derby and to become prime minister. He achieved all three. When he resigned as leader of the Liberal Party, Gladstone made an assessment of Rosebery's character: 'I can say three things of him: one, he is one of the very ablest men I have ever known; two, he is of the highest honour and probity; and three, I do not know whether he really has common sense.'

Halfway up the Lough I looked back at Belfast and imagined how the formidable shipyards, linen mills and rope works must have looked from the boat in the eyes of Billy's young parents, about to put down their roots in this part of the world.

Our sailing took just over three hours and the weather and conditions were perfect. We disembarked just after lunchtime and began the long drive to Cockermouth in Cumbria, across the border. The road had been improved since the last time I was on it, in my teens, almost thirty years ago, furiously driving through the night, my girlfriend beside me, as Stevie Wonder's song 'Superwoman' kept fading in and out on Radio Luxembourg. Billy is naturally garrulous and kept me occupied, but in between the silences memories came to me, about old friends, what had happened to them in the Troubles, who had and had not survived, and the journeys we have all gone through.

We were short on petrol but there were no petrol stations (bar two family ones that looked permanently closed) on the seventy-mile stretch between Stranraer and Dumfries. And when we did stop to refuel, across the English border, the garage accepted our Northern Irish sterling notes, though I had expected objections. At that garage and, later, when we asked for directions or ordered coffee and sandwiches in a café or diner, we found the English to be gentle, kind, warm and helpful, without being ingratiating – in sharp contrast to my experience in Ireland of their uniformed sons, and, I believe, to the experience of other subject peoples around the world, who found them repressive, pompous and self-righteous. I wondered how such a cultured and law-abiding people could dramatically change personae when they stepped onto someone else's shore.

Throughout our journey there were to be many literary reminders. We passed through Dumfries, where Robbie Burns spent his last days, and drove past Eccelfechan, birthplace of Thomas Carlyle, the historian and essayist. It was Carlyle who introduced to the English language that brilliant German word *schadenfreude*, to express the perverse pleasure we take in someone's misfortunes. He used it to describe the British Chancellor of the Exchequer, Benjamin Disraeli's delight in mischief when proposing the Second Reform Bill in 1867, which extended the franchise to many city workers and small farmers. (In his younger days Disraeli wrote trashy love novels, which received terrible reviews. It was he who also said: 'There are three kind of lies: lies, damned lies and statistics.')

We arrived at Cockermouth around five o'clock, stopping off at a shop so that Billy could buy some flowers. Gibbie's and Billy's eyes lit up when they saw each other. Gibbie is very nimble for eighty-six, and helped Billy with his things. A Scotsman, Gibbie was born in Coatbridge in 1915. He says that although his town's population was divided fifty-fifty between Protestants and Catholics, he never met a Catholic until he went to university. Billy married Maureen, a Catholic from Ballymacarret, East Belfast. Maureen's mother was a convert from the Protestant faith, and had come from Farnham Street on the Lower Ormeau Road, an area which during recent decades has experienced a complete demographic shift and is now wholly nationalist. It is one of those areas which the Orange Order demands a 'traditional' right to march through several times each year.

Billy worked as a weaver in linen factories in Belfast but devoted all his holiday time to hostelling. Sixty-five years ago, on a July day, in the Scottish village of Balloch, at the bottom of Loch Lomond, he stopped to look in a shop window. Another young man came up and looked into the window, then said to Billy, 'Where are you going?' Billy replied, 'I haven't decided, but I'll go wherever you're going.'

So they hostelled together, were sometimes mistaken for brothers, and forged a lifelong friendship, writing to each other when Gibbie was in the British army during World War II, and visiting each other, even after they were both married. They met their wives, Maureen and Sadie, whilst hostelling: Billy in Slievenamon in the Mourne Mountains, and Gibbie in the Cairngorms. Both Maureen and Sadie died three years before their present meeting, and Billy and Gibbie hadn't seen each other in twelve years.

It was a glorious evening, so we sat on a bench in Gibbie's back garden, and I listened with fascination as they reminisced about their hostel days, trekking on mountains and bogs, about all the characters they went about with, about the 'code', quite chivalrous, that operated in the Youth Hostel Movement in the 1930s, and the respect that young men had for women.

Billy is self-educated and has an amazing grasp of poetry and an impressive repertoire. Although his father read a lot, Billy attributes his interest in books to several influences: his neighbours, the Boyces from Rosebery Road, whose house came down with books and whose sons were among the few working-class people who went on to university (Billy remembers John Hewitt being a regular visitor to their house); and Joe Walker, 'an ingrained socialist' from Newtownards, a moulder in Harlands, just like Billy's father. Walker bought a book every Saturday, and the books crept up the walls of his sitting room like ivy, as he had no shelves.

Gibbie has a degree in English from Glasgow University and worked as a teacher before retiring. He never expected to end his days in Cockermouth. When World War II broke out, a friend of his from Coatbridge, a law clerk who was working his way up to be a solicitor, refused to serve and declared himself a conscientious objector. He was sent to Barlinnie Prison in Scotland, where harsh treatment eventually broke him. He then agreed to join the army but when he went for his medical he was turned down – due to a mastoid infection in his ear from childhood. Instead of going to war, he relieved an employee from a legal practice in Aberdeen who went off to fight. On one occasion the clerk was sent to investigate a claim in the Lake District and whilst there he met a nurse from South Wales, fell in love and eventually married. He always spoke to Gibbie about the beauty of the Lake District but Gibbie was too proud, or too Scottish, he says, to take it in. Then, when Gibbie's daughter Margaret got married and moved to Cockermouth, he and Sadie came to live there – the place about which he was once dismissive – in order to be near her. Although millions have experienced displacement due to war and conflict, or have had to emigrate from their native country, I suppose that the majority of people in this world live and die close to the land or village or street where they were born.

On Wednesday the three of us went for a drive through part of the Lake District, past lakes whose names I, as a kid, had to learn in geography class, along with details of the British coal and steel industries. The scenery was breathtaking but the countryside was fairly deserted of livestock and visitors due to the outbreak of foot-and-mouth disease, which had hit Cumbria quite hard. We drove past many roadside inns and hotels and I often wondered if this or that one was where Roy and Vera had stayed, thirty years before.

Whether in reference to nature or the elements, love or life, Billy or Gibbie would recite part of a verse from Wordsworth, who was born in Cockermouth, or Burns, or the Bible, and the other would finish it. I couldn't keep up with them and I wished I had a tape recorder.

> Early sun on Beaulieu water
> Lights the undersides of oaks,
> Clumps of leaves it floods and blanches,
> All transparent glow the branches
> Which the double sunlight soaks.

I asked Billy where he got that from and he replied, 'Betjeman, "Youth and Age on Beaulieu River, Hants".' Later, I looked up the poem and learnt that it was about mortality and an old woman's envy of a young girl.

Over the past year Billy has increasingly been talking about death. He becomes emotional when talking about his son Bill, a talented craftsman, who died suddenly of a heart attack three years ago. He says how much he misses Maureen, who died from cancer, and talks about her deep Catholic faith and belief in the afterlife, which he could never share. He talks about his youth, about Rosebery Road, to which I've offered to bring him, but which he does not want to see. And he wonders whether he'll make it to ninety.

Billy was the youngest of three sons and four daughters, the rest of whom are now dead (John, Alexander, Molly, Edith, Nellie and Mamie). He said to me once, 'All the sisters got married and left. It was a tremendous regret to see your family diminishing like that. Everything changes so horribly as you grow up. All of them are gone . . . I am the last of the Mohicans.'

The McCullochs (from left): Molly, Edith, John William (father),
John, Alexander, Billy, Mary Francis (mother), Nelly, Mamie

He pointed to an old family picture on the wall, taken
around 1919. 'There's my father sitting there,' he said, 'and
you can tell by his attitude that he was the disciplinarian of
the family. My mother was a very, very soft person. I can
never remember my mother chastising me in any way. I was a
spoilt skitter! But I loved my oul' mother and you can see by
the photograph that I'm hanging on to her there.'

I had asked him some questions about his parents' court-
ship, the type of detail that a child might pick up from
innuendo or banter in the home, but he couldn't recall. 'I
can't even ask my sisters, who are bound to know a hell of a
lot more about my mother and father than I would . . . Damn
it, it's bloody awful when they're all gone. They used to live
over in different parts of East Belfast and you'd go over there
and you'd say, I'll go and see Molly. Ah Christ, she's dead.
Bloody awful,' he whispered through clenched teeth.

Driving around Derwent Water, Billy and Gibbie had the cheek
to sing and exchange hymns, and I joked with them because
they are both atheists. In St George's Church in High Street,
Belfast, Billy's father had been an 'official'; that is, he organised
the collection at the Church of Ireland services, and through
him, Billy and his brother, John, became members of the choir.
However, Billy claims that he himself was 'a crow', and bluffed
his way for some time. Then, one day at school, an inspector

came into his class and asked his teacher, Miss Freebourne, if she had any good singers. 'I knew right away what she was going to say. She said, "Willie, could you sing something for the inspector?" Well, I fell from grace after that.' Nevertheless, he dates his love of classical music to that time.

His brother John was known in the family as a 'joiner' – not by trade but because he would have joined anything. He was an engineer at the shipyard, joined the merchant navy, then joined the Orange Order on his return. Billy joked that he must have taken after his brother. The parents of Billy's companion Robert Boyce were members of the Plymouth Brethren and Billy used to go along to the meeting hall with them. He recalled one preacher, a bread-server, who used to get up and do his stint, beginning, 'Dear Brethren and Cistern . . . ' which had Robert and Billy wetting themselves.

As a young boy, Billy also had the distinction of marching down the Lower Ormeau Road with the Orange Order. An Orangeman called Jimmy, who was dating Billy's sister Mimi, asked him would he like to carry a string of one of the banners on the Twelfth of July parade. 'Says I, "Do I get paid?"' 'Certainly, you get paid,' he was assured. And he did.

Gibbie directed us to Pendle Hill and showed me the rock where George Fox, the founder of the Quaker Movement, had preached to thousands of people in the 1650s. 'When I was come to the top, I saw the sea bordering Lancashire. From the top of this hill the Lord let me see in what places he had a great people to be gathered. As I went down, I found a spring of water in the side of the hill, with which I refreshed myself, having eaten or drunk but little for several days before.'

Fox was imprisoned eight times between 1649 and 1675. He met Cromwell in 1656 and advised him not to accept the crown which was being offered to him and which he eventually refused. Fox argued against the formalism of the established Church and all social conventions: 'The Lord forbade me to put off my hat to any, high or low . . . neither might I bow or scrape my leg to anyone.'

Billy, Gibbie and I had our last supper together on Wednesday night. I cooked, as they again sat outside in the warm evening, close together, retelling events from forty and fifty years ago, cracking open small epiphanies to reveal what one or other had perhaps forgotten, and I heard the occasional laugh and confirmation.

On Thursday morning, Billy (left, above) and Gibbie came out to the car and I asked them to stand for a photograph. They shook hands for a long time and said goodbye. As we turned the corner from Rose Lane, Billy said with finality and passion, 'That's my old friend Gibbie, whom I met in 1936.'

> Thus far, O Friend! have we, though leaving much
> Unvisited, endeavoured to retrace
> The simple ways in which my childhood walked;
> Those chiefly that first led me to the love
> Of rivers, woods, and fields . . .
>
> O Friend! O Poet! brother of my soul,
> Think not that I could pass along untouched
> By these remembrances.

WILLIAM WORDSWORTH

BOB CONKLIN

At dinner on Sunday afternoons, some light music from other eras plays in the background, which suits the mood and my love of nostalgia. Last Remembrance Sunday, many of the songs and melodies on the radio were from the two world wars: 'As Time Goes By', 'White Cliffs of Dover', 'Over There', 'My Sweetheart is Somewhere in France', and 'It's a Long, Long Way to Tipperary'.

As we finished eating, Billy recalled receiving the news of his older brother Alex, who served in the Royal Horse Artillery in the First World War, being wounded in action, albeit not seriously. And he remembered the day that he, aged seven, was playing in the backyard when his mother suddenly startled him: 'She was peeling potatoes and heard the news. She threw her knife and the potato into the air and squealed, "The war's over! The war's over!"'

My wife, Leslie, went upstairs and returned with some old photographs, one of which featured a handsome young man, Private Bob (Robert) Conklin, her great-uncle from Toronto, who fought with the Canadian Corps in France in 1918. She told us that her mother Sheila and Aunt Nancy still had Bob's letters and one of his diaries.

A few months later, on holiday in Toronto, I asked to see Bob's papers, which included many photographs of him and his comrades, postcards he had sent home and newspaper clippings which his family had gathered and cherished. Again, as when going through the relics of the dead in Altaghoney, I felt honoured and handled these precious documents with care. I could hear Bob's filial voice addressing his parents, Laura and James, and his gentle advice, that of a 'big brother', to his younger siblings, Veny (Evelyn), Alfred, Norman, Isabel and Dorothy. The letters give a vivid account of his experiences. 'I try to make my letters interesting when I have something to talk about or describe,' he says in one.

Bob was the eldest child in the family. He won a scholarship every year between 1910 and 1914, and at the end of the final year headed his class. He could speak some French and quote Browning, and wrote a few pieces of light-hearted verse about army life. He worked for the Merchants Bank in Toronto before enlisting in 1916 at the age of eighteen.

He was in love with Isobel Howes, to whom he was engaged, jokingly referred to her as his 'wife', and pasted photographs of her into his diary, creating a little picture gallery. Through the *Toronto Star* newspaper I tried to discover if Bob's many letters to Isobel – from Camp Borden Training Camp, from England and the western front – were still extant, but learnt from one of her relatives, Alan Welch, a nephew, that Isobel's last surviving and youngest brother, Edwin, had died just a year earlier, aged eighty-eight. Alan had no recollection of any of Bob's letters and so the trail went cold.

Much of Bob's earlier correspondence expresses his frustration at the delay in going over to England and the monotonous training and endless drilling and marching. Then, in his diary in February 1917 he writes:

Lt. Col. Cooper announced to the Buffs [Canadian Buffs, 198th Battalion, Canadian Expeditionary Forces] that we would leave Friday. Great was the rejoicing. Wednesday will be our last free day. Home for dinner. Down town and bought a vanity case for Isobel . . . To Isobel's for supper. We went out for a walk. A very mild night.

Sunday

Isobel and I went to church and heard a good sermon. Left about 11.45 and came back to camp. Our time grows shorter.

Monday

Isobel was in for supper and the evening . . . One hears nothing these days but our departure. We are beginning to realise that we are going.

Tuesday

Isobel and I went to Shea's in evening and saw a dandy show . . . Went home from Isobel's and had a good bed. Rather tired and could not sleep for a time.

Thursday

In camp. Visitors allowed in. Father and mother, Evelyn, Minnie and Hubbie, Rubie and Isobel down. Two bright spots in our goodbye. Mother acted like a trump and we parted all serene. Saw Ben Cameron's aunts. The friendship between Isobel and me entered a new stage, at least from my viewpoint and feeling.

Friday

After a lot of deliberation I phoned Isobel and had a nice talk. Our train left at 3 o'clock. Father carried my two kit bags – one filled with kit and one with eats. Also had a big box from home. Sorry to leave home but it is time we went.

He was among two thousand troops who boarded the *Meta-gama* in Halifax, bound for Liverpool. Even before they left, they suffered their first casualty.

> A most unfortunate accident occurred tonight. Steve Kerr, one of the men in Seven Platoon, fell down a hatchway and broke his neck. He died very soon after. Just how the thing happened nobody appears to know definitely. A boxing match had gathered a crowd and he either tried to pass the crowd or attempted to get a better view by getting on the railing around the hatch. At any rate, he fell in. He was a dandy chap – a real gentleman and well liked by all the boys.

They watched as other boats set sail for England.

> We were peacefully eating our supper when the *Lapland* steamed slowly down the harbour past us. We lost no time in finishing our meal and getting out on the deck. The *Southland*, with decks lined with troops and bands playing, passed soon after. They cheered and we answered heartily. About 5.15 we began to turn our nose towards the sea and then we knew we were off.
>
> Slowly we steamed down the harbour, cheering as we passed a small boat, or in answer to a crowd on a dock . . . Our band played "Rule Britannia" as we passed and we got a great cheer. The echo was none the less hearty . . .
>
> Gradually we gained speed and the land grew dim until about seven o'clock when we saw the shores of Canada melt into the horizon. It made me feel a bit homesick, but that soon passed away. We all began to survey our new surroundings and to encounter the dead roll of the ocean.

In England they faced almost another year of constant preparation and training. Units were broken up and friends separated. One day he wrote to his mother that he had been going through his Bible when he came across a particular passage.

I was reading my Testament and ran across 13:16 of 1 Corinthians. It was marked. Did you do it, mother? I always try to live up to it. [The verse reads: 'Watch ye, stand fast in the faith, quit you like men, be strong.']

On one of his leaves in April 1917, he and his comrade Brock took a train to Bristol and visited the parental home of their friend Jack Pope. He wrote:

We spent the time at Jack's mostly listening to his brother Henry who is attached to the Imperial Service, doing YMCA work at one of the camps. He came over on the *Laconia,* the boat sunk by a sub that really brought USA into the war.

On 25 February 1917, the SS *Laconia,* sailing from New York to England, had been sunk off the coast of Ireland, with the loss of twelve lives. Among its passengers was Floyd Gibbons, the soon-to-be-famed headline hunter and war reporter of the *Chicago Tribune.* His published account of the sinking of the *Laconia* helped change America's isolationist sentiment and pushed it into the declaration of war against Germany that followed in less than two months.

Bob's letter continues:

Henry Pope was in one of the reading rooms when the torpedo struck the stern about ten o'clock on a Sunday evening. He went to his cabin, got his overcoat (he was a civilian then) and went to the lifeboat assigned him. They loaded it and commenced to lower it until one of the other boats got beneath theirs and the boat was stopped until the one beneath got clear. When they recommenced lowering, the ropes fouled and one end refused to move, with the result that the boat gradually tilted and the men began to gradually drop off. When Henry saw this he took hold of a rope and climbed about forty feet onto the deck. He went over the whole deck and the only one left was an old sailor who had decided to go down with the liner. Henry persuaded him to come along and they both looked for some means of saving themselves.

Near the stern they saw a boat slowly moving away. The strong light from the moon made the boat quite visible. By shouting at the top of their lungs they attracted the attention of the sailor in it and it turned back. The next job was to get into the lifeboat. Henry saw a rope hanging from the davit and by a lucky roll of the sinking ship was able to grasp it. Handing it to the sailor he watched him slide down and be hauled in. Then Henry started his slide. It was a drop of sixty feet. His hands were terribly burned but he was hauled into the lifeboat safely.

In his account Floyd Gibbons refers to an old sailor, perhaps the same one: 'Seeking to establish some authority in our boat, I made my way to the stern and there found an old, white-haired sea captain, a second-cabin passenger, with whom I had talked before. He was bound from Nova Scotia with codfish. His sailing schooner, the *Secret*, had broken in two, but he and his crew had been taken off by a tramp and taken back to New York. He had sailed from there on the *Ryndam*, which, after almost crossing the Atlantic, had turned back. The *Laconia* was his third attempt to get home. His name is Captain Dear.'

Bob continued:

For eight hours they tossed about in the open sea with waves towering above them. A [German] submarine rose to the surface and after a few words the commander bade them goodnight and told them the destroyers would pick them up soon. Henry was so sick he could not straighten out. Must have been a terrible eight hours. They, along with nearly all the passengers and crew, were picked up by a destroyer and after twenty-four hours, during which time they were packed so tight that nobody could sit down, they reached a port in Ireland. It must have been a terrible experience.

In the summer of 1917 the closest Bob got to action was taking part as an extra in a propaganda film aimed at the USA public:

Wednesday we carried on with a new part of our training – movie acting . . . We fell in at 8.30 in full marching order and proceeded down the Portsmouth Road where we were photographed by the movie man as we swung along (Scene I). Then we halted, while the scene changed.

INTERMISSION

(While the film is being changed I will tell you of the coming reel. We are an English regiment leaving our home town on the way to the firing line)

SCENE II

The battalion swings around the corner and passes through the village – the streets lined with people (mostly girls collected from the neighbourhood and transported by motor trucks) who wave frantically with hats, handkerchiefs and ferns, and are most liberal with thrown kisses and appealing and entreating glances.

END OF ACT I

We then stopped for dinner and waited while the scenery was arranged for the next act. We went back to the Trench area.

ACT II

The scene: a low ridge to the north: an intervening space of four hundred yards and a high ridge to the south.
The actors: The Germans (Buffs behind the North ridge and wearing hats reversed and advancing in mass formation): the British (the remainder of the Brigade advancing on us in waves).
The action: About thirty mines; gas bombs, smoke bombs – everything that made smoke.

The spectators: half the countryside; Griffiths (the producer of *The Birth of a Nation* and the one we were assisting in), Lillian Gish, the leading lady in the aforementioned movie.

FINIS

It was a very realistic scene and only needed the bullets and shells to make it real. That night it was after six when we got back so we were allowed out until 11.30 in compensation.

In September he wrote again about their frustration:

My dearest Mother,

Another week has rolled by and here we are still in Witley with no signs of a departure in the near future. The possibility is that we are better off here but the training does get monotonous and we do get weary of it . . . On the route march, Friday, one of the boys asked the Colonel, "Will we be in France for Christmas?" and he replied with a grin, "Either in France or in a lunatic asylum." Speaking further, he said it was the Conscription Bill that was holding us back and that if a sufficient number of men were quickly raised in Canada we would not be long in going over . . .

Raining again . . . The wind gradually increased until at midnight it was blowing a gale and for a short time then the rain stopped and for about two minutes the moon came out from behind the dark clouds that were rushing in a wild mass of confusion across the sky. Those short and faint moonbeams revealed a most desolate scene. In even rows lay the shelters, shiny and wet and flapping and tugging on the ropes. The ground was netted with streams, large and small, winding their meandering ways down to the road where they collected and formed a torrent that was carrying sticks, papers and pebbles along in its current. But far more desolate looking than the wild sky or the muddy earth were the drenched groups of men that clustered together in an endeavour to revive drooping spirits with a song or two . . .

What's the use of worrying?
It never was worthwhile. So
Pack all your troubles in your old kitbag
And smile, smile, smile!!!

On another day his unit played the part of the Germans:

Half our men were in German uniforms and the 145th were
all dressed in French costumes of light blue. Smoke bombs,
mines and blank shots made the fighting seem very realistic.
The Scouts and Signallers made a raid and we nearly all
died beautifully in all manner of fashions on the way to the
French front line. It was my place to try and run back and
get shot in doing so.

In December 1917 he learned that a friend of his father has
offered to help him take out a 'commission', which might
have allowed him to avoid going to the front. Bob wrote
back to his mother:

Please have Father convey to Mr Moore my appreciation
of the interest he has taken in me and also of the
generosity he has shown in offering to help me take out a
commission. Having come so far I would not like to make
any move in that direction now. I would sooner have a
try at the life in France and then consider the matter. I
understand that after a few months' active service it is
not a difficult matter for a good man to take out a
commission – if the OC will recommend it. Thank Mr
Moore very sincerely for me.

On Christmas Day he writes:

Hello everybody. A Merry Christmas? Yes, I've had a good
time – not as pleasant as I had last year, or as good as I hope
to have next year – but I managed to enjoy myself . . .

One box came on Christmas Day and that from Isobel. It was a beauty – all tied up with white paper and decorated with red tabs. It contained socks, wristlets, handkerchiefs, cake, gum, maple sugar, pork and beans and a silk handkerchief from Eva Sexton . . . I spent the afternoon quietly, writing to Isobel.

He describes the scene in the camp as 1918 begins:

Very few went to bed before the New Year came in. At 11.55 PM, 31 December 1917, the bugle band sounded the last post, ushering out the Old Year; and at 12.01 AM, 1 January 1918, they played reveille to awaken the New Year. Then, after exchanging best wishes amongst the boys of the section we crawled under the sheets.

Thus entered 1918 with us in Witley Camp. I wonder where the incoming of 1919 will find us? We know where we would like to be and here's hoping our wishes and desires will come true in that regard . . .

Tell the kiddies I send my love.

Then comes the day:

Mother and Dad,
The news this letter will convey is not very cheering to you but the inevitable must come. The 5th Canadian Division is no more. RIP! The Buffs have been called upon for a draft of 400 men – 100 from each Company . . . I have been transferred to B Coy along with the original 201st boys . . . Ben and I and all the boys mentioned are in the first draft to the 19th [Battalion, 4th Brigade, 2nd Canadian Division] and we expect to move inside a week...

Everybody is on the move and we're all worked up fit to kill. Those inclined are celebrating in a manner that does not help them to walk straight and the hut has been a case of 'Bedlam let loose' . . . Our kits were carefully examined this morning and we were supposed to carry on with our Lewis gun work, but the 'draft fever' was too high and we did very little. Everyone is happy as a lark . . . Don't worry now, I am on the same job as the rest and am taking the same chance as the rest of the boys...We are all pleased to think that we are going to do our bit.

In another letter he writes:

My dear Father . . . I expect that we will leave the day after next from Milford for service in France. After reveille this morning we are on a minute's notice and I expect tonight will be our last free night . . . Hereafter, I suppose I'll have to think over each sentence I am to write for fear I say something which will offend the censor . . .

'I don't want you to begin worrying now that I am going out to do my bit. The majority of my friends and acquaintances who have seen service have gone through it safely and I see no reason why I should be less fortunate.

'I realize that all the anxiety rests with those at home, for, while we all long to be back again, we all have a duty to perform and the cost matters not.

His battalion is transported to France and he writes that he is in the rifle grenade section of the platoon.

Today, Sunday, I am on guard and am writing this on my knee. I am wondering if you will ever be able to make it out. The pen is dry and I have no ink handy so I'm obliged to use indelible pencil . . . News (that may pass the censor) is scarce and I only wish I could tell you all I want to about what I have seen.

He was moved up to the front in early April and writes about the German bombardment that greeted them. They sleep during the day and work at night, 'carrying rations, digging trenches and generally improving our own line.' Bob was only ten days at the front when the Conklins received a telegram regretting to inform them that he had been wounded. Due to the delay in the post from France it was some weeks before they heard from Bob himself, to say that he had been hit by shrapnel and was recovering in hospital. As he improved, he helped out on the ward and then was placed on guard duty. However, he was anxious to get back to the front:

> This may seem foolish with me having a 'bomb proof' here, but, you know, misery loves company, so we may as well face the music together. At any rate I've had a good trip down the line, and I can have another try at my luck . . . Can you send me a clipping from the *Telegram* or *Star* telling about my casualty? Or have you already and it hasn't reached me? I'd like to see my picture in print.

In the spring of 1918 the German General Ludendorff, who determined the strategy on the Western Front, staked all on a massive offensive, which was initially successful but then began unravelling. In July, Bob wrote:

> The news these last few days has been very encouraging and everybody is quite confident that the Commander-in-Chief, Foch, will be able to give the Huns the drubbing they deserve. With the Yanks coming over in such large numbers the allies should soon be able to force the issue. There isn't much to report. All is quiet on our front and the spirit of the troops is excellent . . . Surely Kaiser Bill can see that it is useless for him to go any further. I don't think it will be many months longer before the Hun decides he has had enough.

On 8 August, nine days before Bob was posted back to the front, the Canadian Corps, 100,000 strong, attacked the enemy and drove the Germans back a distance of thirteen kilometres. Ludendorff described 8 August as 'the blackest day of the German army in the history of the war'. He offered his resignation but the Kaiser refused it, though the Kaiser had by then made the decision that 'the war must be ended'.

On 26 August, the 4th Canadian Brigade, including Bob's unit, took part in the battle for Arras, at the northern edge of the Somme salient. The assault was launched at 3 AM. The 4th Brigade moved rapidly through the enemy's outpost zone and reached the outskirts of Guemappe where they came under heavy shelling. At an unknown hour, somewhere between Guemappe and Monchy, Bob was wounded again and removed to a casualty clearing station. In three days of fighting, the 2nd and 3rd Divisions lost 254 officers and 5,547 other ranks.

On 6 September, Bob's twenty-first birthday, his mother received a telegram from the Director of Records:

Mrs Laura Conklin, 418 Euclid Ave Toronto Ont. 3331 Deeply regret inform you 228305 Pte. Robert James Davidson Conklin infantry officially reported died of wounds 1 casualty clearing station August 29th gunshot wound back.

Eerily, two days later they heard from Bob. It was a letter, dated 11 August:

Our cushy job is finished and I am taking another trip up to fire a few more rounds at Heine . . . We are all pleased at the recent news, especially as the Canadians have figured in it. We seem to have Heine on the go now and perhaps we can keep him that way . . .

Give my love to all, and don't worry on my account . . . I am enclosing a bit of white heather from Bonnie Scotland. It's lucky – let's hope for both sender and recipient.

Another letter arrived, dated 15 August:

> This morning we did some salvaging and I found this pad –
> and the ink (which, I may say, is of Heine manufacture and
> was found in one of his old dug-outs) . . . I received a few
> letters yesterday . . . None came from Isobel but it is very
> likely down-the-line looking for me there . . .

After his death, three more letters arrived, his last to his sister
Veny [Evelyn], dated 22 August:

> It is a scorching hot day, but I am thankful to say that I am
> stretched out on the grass 'in the shade of the old apple
> tree'. There is a faint breeze blowing at times, and it is much
> enjoyed I assure you.
>
> Now my dear 'kid sister, who is Eighteen', I have
> written you a letter, but there is one thing lacking that is
> essential for a good letter and that is news, and just as
> you have meatless, heatless and eatless days, we have our
> newsless days. But some day I'll be able to say what I would
> like to, I think, if all goes well, and then there won't be
> any need to close as follows: Well, my news is finished, so
> I'll ring off.
>
> PS I will write Mother in a few days. Love to all. Bob.

He never got to write that letter.

Bob Conklin, along with 632 Commonwealth soldiers and
46 German soldiers, is buried in Ligny-St Flochel cemetery,
France. Five weeks after his death Germany sent out her first
peace note and World War I ended with the armistice on the
eleventh hour of the eleventh day of the eleventh month,
1918.

Two photographs were found on Bob when he was killed
and were returned to the family. One is of his mother and his
sisters Veny and Isabel, feeding some chicks, taken in June
1918 at their holiday home at Rosebank on the shore of Lake

Ontario. The other is of Isobel Howes. On the back of the photo she has written: 'How do you like my "wedding" clothes?'

A year after his death a sympathy notice appeared in a Toronto newspaper:

CONKLIN – Sacred to the memory of Pte. R. J. D. Conklin, who enlisted with the 201st Battalion and was transferred to 198th Buffs Battalion, died 29 Aug 1918, at Battle of Arras, buried at Ligny-St Flochel.

> Not now, but in the coming years,
> It may be in the Better Land
> We'll read the meaning of our tears
> And then, up there, we'll understand.
>
> We'll know why clouds instead of sun
> Were over many a cherished plan.
> Why song had ceased when scarce begun
> 'Tis then, up there, we'll understand.

FAMILY

In 1919 Bob's fiancée, Isobel, broken-hearted since his death some months earlier, but continuing her work as a nurse, perished in the Spanish influenza epidemic that killed 50,000 Canadians and millions worldwide.

Once a Volunteer

Paul was handsome, despite some crooked teeth, and a good footballer, but I didn't like him. I thought he threw his weight around too much, and was too cocky. We were second years in the same form, aged around twelve, and our class was queuing up on the top landing waiting to go in to Latin.

Each landing was inset a little from the main front windows by a rail. Thus, you could look at the landing below and see the schoolboys lining up at the rail there. Paul leaned over the balcony, allowed a big dollop of spittle to collect on the end of his tongue and then snipped it with his lips. A first year down below cried that he had been spat on and Paul laughed.

At that moment Brother Gibbons, our Latin teacher, who was also the vice-principal, a tall, gaunt-faced and violent man, was just passing the first years. He took the rest of the stairs at three at a time and ordered us to our desks. He said that what had happened was despicable and that the culprit should come forward or else the entire class (of about thirty-two pupils) would get 'six of the best' from his cane. He must have lectured us for about thirty-five minutes about the issue, about how the young kid felt, how the boy responsible was really a coward. He said it was impossible that none of us had seen the culprit. He said he would give us a chance. We were told to write down on bits of paper who we knew or thought had done it. It would be completely anonymous.

After lunch Gibbons recalled the class. Gibbons announced that he knew the culprit but would give him one more chance to act like a man. If he didn't come forward, he would regret it. There was silence. Paul grew pale. He was told to stand.

Gibbons let him stew for a few moments before calling him to the top of the class. He accused him of spitting on the first year. He brooked no contradiction. Paul cried and said he didn't do it. We knew he knew he was going to get caned. But Brother Gibbons simply said to him, 'Go back to your desk.' Paul returned uncertainly and proceeded to sit down. 'Now,' said Gibbons, 'leave your books but take your bag, and get out of my school. You are a disgrace; you are dismissed. Now, go home and tell your mother and father why I dismissed you!'

I couldn't believe it. To be dismissed was about the worst thing that could befall you. Paul tried to say something but Gibbons raised his voice: 'Out! Get out!'

Afterwards, everybody was speculating about who squealed on Paul. I squirmed in the vicinity of these conversations because it was I who had written down Paul's full name. I don't know if I was the only one. Gibbons had collected this lottery before letting us out to the dining hall. After dinner Gibbons collared me beside the lockers. I was shocked: he had recognised my handwriting, which I had tried to disguise.

He said, 'Are you sure it's him! Are you sure!'

I whimpered, 'Yes.' All that night I was miserable and despised myself. I couldn't sleep. But my agony was relieved the following day when discussions between Paul's mother and the principal saw him back in class. We later became good friends but I never told him, or anyone, that I had been the informer.

I used the incident when I wrote my first novel, *West Belfast*, which was published just before I was arrested in January 1990 and charged with conspiracy to murder Sandy Lynch, a police informer. Only one reader took any notice of the hero, John O'Neill's informing on his classmate: the OC of the IRA in Crumlin Road Jail, Seanna Walsh. 'Um,' he said with a smile. 'That's interesting. So, it was *he* who squealed on Paul McShane.'

That experience at school made me distrustful of authority and highly conscious of the consequences of my actions. I determined to keep secret anything that I was told in confidence, a rule I have broken in certain of my writings when I felt that circumstances had changed (usually through a death) and that harm or hurt would be minimal and outweighed by the value of revelation and truth.

When the Troubles broke out and I was first tempted to join the IRA the fear of not being able to withstand interrogation, to be able to keep secrets, stayed my hand. My conversion to physical force came slowly.

I had been at some protests called by People's Democracy. As I said earlier, my transmitter (amongst others) was one of those used to broadcast Radio Free Belfast when republicans got organised after 15 August 1969. A photograph of me and another young person at the controls was published in the *Irish News* in early September. That autumn at school I sold raffle tickets to raise money for the defence of our area. As the split in the IRA proceeded, I sided with those colloquially known as the 'Provies'.

At the early riots I was a bystander, not a participant. From 1970 I had sold *Republican News* from underneath my coat outside Mass but it was only after the British army curfew of the Falls Road in July 1970 that I decided to go one step further and hold guns for the IRA on the understanding that they were for defensive purposes only.

A friend approached me. He said that he had been holding a dump for the IRA but that some neighbours had got to know about it. The IRA wanted to move it and asked him did he know anyone who would hold it for a few weeks. I thought about it and then agreed. My family was on holiday in England and I had the house to myself. Two days later a young fella, acting as a scout, came to my back door, which I had opened as arranged, and a minute later a man in his early twenties arrived, carrying a big guitar case. I immediately liked the young fella, and he and I stood talking about politics and pop music. The IRA man decided the best place for the guns was under the floorboards on the landing. We lifted the carpets. The boards had been hammered down so tightly that he needed to saw through them. But even then the rifle was still too long to fit in. I suggested just leaving them in the case and putting them under my bunk bed. My mother allowed me to look after and clean my own bedroom. I had kept diaries in a drawer and knew that there had been no intrusion. I assured them it would be okay, the weapons would be safe. Of course, after they left I had to make a full inspection. Besides the .303 Lee Enfield rifle, there were a Sterling sub-machine gun, a Luger pistol, bags of magazines and loose ammunition, and two hand grenades. I worked out how to assemble and load the weapons and I imagined being in a gun battle, prepared to kill or die. After three or four inspections the novelty of handling guns wore off and I packed them away under the bed, placing various boxes of books in front of the guitar case. I couldn't sleep for the first week or two, but then became accustomed to the presence of the dump and sometimes forgot about it altogether.

We were one of the few families in our area still friendly with British soldiers. None had yet been shot by the IRA. There were weekends when soldiers who were on leave came and stayed with us. They bunked with me, separated by the mattress from an IRA arms dump. It felt odd and exciting being in command of a great secret – and appreciating the irony of the situation. But I also felt guilty, because deep down I knew my father would be driven out of his job in the telephone exchange if ever the house were raided. Still, I took a liberty with his liberty, squared it in my conscience that somebody had to hold these guns, and deluded myself into thinking that my accepting full responsibility for them in the event of a raid would exonerate him.

A greater fear was what I would say under interrogation, because over the following weeks I had learnt the identities of the two IRA Volunteers involved in putting the guns in my house.

One Saturday I boarded a bus on the Falls Road to go into town, and as it passed my street I saw the British army begin raiding houses. I got off at the next stop and walked back, expecting the arms to be discovered. I prepared myself for arrest and kept repeating that I would not give the names of those who had left them. After a few house searches the army stopped short of ours and left the street. I thanked God. One night in January 1971 the IRA came and asked for the guitar case and I was relieved to see it go.

Any moral resistance I had to violence was being rapidly undermined by the actions of the British army and the RUC during and after the introduction of internment. One problem I had with supporting war is that in taking the life of an enemy one couldn't be sure that that person was the particular soldier or police officer who revelled in oppression and was personally responsible for violence and death. But that is part of a universal paradox: in most wars good people kill good people for separate and opposite perceived good causes, in a narrative which includes heroism, cowardice, cruelty and rapine, which ends in triumph, or negotiation and compromise – only for a later generation to go out and slaughter again. And this is even before one considers another universal: that it is civilians who by and large bear the brunt of suffering. We know this, yet we are helpless.

That autumn, as I studied less and less, against a background of bombs and gun battles, of neighbours being rounded up and interned, or shot, of soldiers stopping you on the street and abusing you, I still hesitated about committing myself, mainly out of a fear that I would give information under interrogation, that I was a coward at heart.

But I was pulled increasingly towards the IRA and their fundamentalist position, and it was more with relief than fear that I took the plunge. Little did I know that a young local IRA Volunteer, when stopped by British army patrols, was keeping them abreast of events and passing on the names of new recruits. I received word from the prison ship *Maidstone* that during the interrogation of a prisoner the RUC had asked about me. Two months later the IRA arrested the young suspect and he admitted being an informer. He was banished from Ireland.

Over the years I've been arrested on many occasions, and held for short periods of a few days or a week, and although never tortured I was threatened, abused and punched about. In one barracks a soldier stubbed out a cigarette on my neck and I was thrown down stairs. But I was never beaten so severely as to discover how relatively low or high my threshold for pain was. I harbour a strong suspicion that my life, self-confidence and reputation could but for the grace of God have been very different.

There is a novel by Arthur Koestler, *Arrival and Departure* (1943), which examines the fine line between heroism and cowardice and counterpoises political commitment against personal happiness. The main character, Peter Slavek, becomes a student hero after surviving interrogation by torture. Under torture he is screaming and the police, concerned that passers-by in the street above will hear, stuff a sponge in his mouth to muffle the noise, unaware that he is on the verge of breaking. Later, he says, 'I have betrayed, though nobody knows it.'

Most people will draw a distinction between someone who breaks under torture, ill treatment, duress or psychological pressure, and someone who goes further and agrees to collaborate. Many people who sign confessions and in-criminate others do so out of a temporary collapse of their convictions in the intimidating atmosphere of an interrogation centre. Once out of that atmosphere, facing and admitting the truth to friends and comrades is the road to self-discovery and, often, greater courage.

Ireland's long struggle for independence from its near neighbour, England, has often been frustrated and undermined by the actions of informers. One person can do a great deal of damage, just like one assassin. When Gavrilo Princip shot and killed Archduke Ferdinand in Sarajevo in 1914, it sparked off the First World War.

Like other conquered countries, Ireland reserved its greatest repugnance not for the enemy, but for one of its own. There is an old saying that sums up the horror of realising that one has been betrayed from within: 'Do you know what the trees say when the axe comes into the forest? Look! The handle is one of us!'

IRA Volunteers had to be paranoid about treachery if they were to survive. Throughout the conflict in the North, the IRA shot dead many men and women whom it accused of secretly working for the British army or the Royal Ulster Constabulary, and banished from Ireland hundreds of others who were discovered before they could cause major damage, or who availed of IRA amnesties.

Who were these informers? The young lad across the street who was caught on a burglary or in a stolen car or in possession of drugs and was promised he would not be charged if he spied on certain neighbours; a husband discovered having an affair with another man's wife and who was vulnerable to police blackmail; and IRA Volunteers too ashamed to admit that they had broken in the barracks. In one case in Derry, where an IRA arms dump was discovered in the house of two sympathisers, the RUC arrested both husband and wife and threatened to charge the woman. They dropped the threat in return for the husband, Paddy Flood, joining the IRA and sabotaging operations. He did so. The IRA eventually flushed him out and killed him, dumping his body on a border road.

All informers have had to enter into contemptible deals, purportedly to save the lives of some, but which endangered the lives of others – and their own – and risked disgracing their families and breaking their hearts.

In recent years some informers have gone public and became media celebrities. They have written mostly atrocious, self-justificatory accounts of their actions and claimed that they were ideological or moral converts to the anti-IRA crusade. (However, even a former head of the RUC Special Branch, Ian Phoenix, dismissed that as nonsense.) Few activists ever willingly went over to the other side, though, undoubtedly, some of those who did enjoyed the financial blandishments – and perhaps the dangers, also.

Some surviving informers are now demanding that any outstanding IRA threat against them be lifted, that they be allowed to return home because of the peace process. I think they should be free to come back, though I don't believe they are really that anxious to return. Who would want to talk to them or sit next to them in a bar or restaurant? Can they explain why they betrayed working-class people, their best friends and relatives; had them arrested, had them killed; broke up families, caused suffering and loss running into many years; protracted the conflict (because republicans were never going to surrender or give in to repression, including the work of informers) – and all because it was they themselves who were weak and pathetic and took blood money from the British and perversely tried to make of betrayal something noble.

The truth – and they know it – is you can never go back, never undo the hurt, never be the self you were before you betrayed your people.

Eamonn Collins, who wrote probably the best and most disturbing account of his times in, and then against, the IRA, *Killing Rage*, did come home. Ironically, there is a close parallel to Gypo Nolan's mental state in Liam O'Flaherty's *The Informer* and Collins's in *Killing Rage*. Collins, even though he had been through a phase as a renegade, a potential supergrass, often reverted to a republican mentality, as if he had forgotten what he had done. Gypo, after he has been exposed as an informer and has escaped from the Organisation, sees two policemen whom he could easily run to for protection. However, 'he still regarded them as his enemies. His mentality had not yet accustomed itself to the change that his going into the police station that evening had wrought in his condition. To his understanding he was still a revolutionary. He was not at all conscious of being an informer, or a friend of law and order . . . '

Collins's temerity in returning to Newry not only to live among those he had accused (and who were arrested and jailed), but to continue to appear on television and radio and level accusations at republicans one day, only to attempt a balanced analysis of republicanism, like a republican spokesperson, the next, was reckless. Early in 1999, while out walking his dog in the early hours, he was viciously beaten to death by unknown assailants on a country road in South Armagh. Did he care about his life any more? Why else make himself available? The sane thing would have been to put the head down.

Some informers, including men who I met in prison, having come forward to the IRA at the time of amnesties or because their consciences overwhelmed them, have been able to live out their lives quietly in Belfast or in other parts of Ireland, unhindered and unknown to the general public. I cannot understand why an informer, having gone over to the other side, would want to come home and risk, at the minimum, ostracism and obloquy and, worse, an execution or fatal assault.

The peace process challenges many of our convictions. There are calls for forgiveness. I realise that for many in the opposite camp my part in struggle is unforgivable.

I always liked to think that I could easily forgive, that I would be indifferent, for example, to the return of Sandy Lynch, the informer who gave evidence against me and others. I was disturbed last year by my reaction to an incident in a Belfast restaurant. My wife and I had been out for a meal when a journalist whom she once worked with came over to our table. He had been at an RUC detective's funeral earlier that day, had been drinking and said that he had been talking to Detective Inspector Tim McGregor, who had taken his severance pay and was retiring to the south of France. He said the inspector wanted to give me a present.

Tim McGregor had charged me in 1990 with conspiracy to murder Sandy Lynch. I liked him even before he first spoke to me. He was very gentle when he took my fingerprints. On a number of subsequent occasions in the prison and in court he asked me how I was keeping and I felt he was sincere. I don't know if he has any blood on his hands or dark secrets, because, let's face it, war is not for the faint-hearted. It is hard to believe that the inept or the ineffectual could occupy and maintain for long a senior position in an organisation such as the RUC. Or that the naive, the honourable or the pure and innocent could become involved in a conflict situation and survive, without being compromised or tainted.

As we finished our meal, the journalist returned and announced that Tim and a party had arrived and they would love us to join them for a glass of wine. He had obviously phoned him. I do not like to be ill-mannered but my wife and I felt very uncomfortable. We finished up and paid the bill. I led the way over to their table at a window beside the exit. Tim stood up and we shook hands. He introduced me to his wife, Joyce, then another woman, then another detective (whose name I forget). They asked us to join them. I said I couldn't. The journalist said, 'Come on! Sure the war's over and we can all be friends now.' I repeated that I couldn't, that the time was not right.

Tim intervened and said, 'I've got something for you.' He handed me a wrapped object, which I opened. It was the court artist's painting of me as I was giving evidence from the witness box, which was used on television to illustrate our trial. It was framed. It was not a very glamorous impression; in fact, compared to it, in real life I looked ten years younger, as if it, like Dorian Gray's painting, was the one growing older. But, as my mother would say, it's the thought that counts. 'I got that after the trial,' he said, 'and kept it for you.'

The journalist asked us to stay once again, but Tim said he understood. 'Off the record,' I said, with a solemn face, just as we were leaving, 'where exactly is Sandy Lynch living these days?'

They laughed. Very good, said the other detective.

I wished Tim well in his retirement and left with his present and promised to send him a copy of my book, *Then The Walls Came Down*, which is based on my prison letters and in which I mention him.

Why did I not sit down?

I felt that their confidence in having me, with my reputation, at their table vaguely suggested the magnanimity of the victor. I felt that the bonhomie was tenuous and that conviviality with former enemies, for whom I feel no bitterness, suggested not quite collaboration, but could be misunderstood by republicans and my community as my having potentially compromised myself.

But what I thought about most was the dead: theirs, in the broadest sense, whom we had killed, and ours, in the broadest sense, whom they had killed – as if the dead were sitting in judgement with their mortal prejudices, looking down on us and saying how dare you, how could you, did our sacrifices amount to nothing, did our suffering and death and manner of death not matter?

THE QUIGLEY BROTHERS

On sunny afternoons after school, my friends and I sat against the gable of the barber's shop at the corner of Beechmount Avenue, eyeing the girls from St Rose's, St Dominic's and St Louisa's making their way home. Two of the lads played guitars, to which we sang Eric Clapton and Fleetwood Mac songs. A few times I noticed a tall youth with a schoolbag over his back dander through the entry opposite us and I instantly recognised him as the fella who had put the guns in my house back in July. One day I winked at him conspiratorially and he smiled back.

Shortly afterwards I left St Mary's Grammar School, where I had been unhappy, and switched to St Peter's Secondary School, and it was there, in the library, that I again met sixteen-year-old Jimmy Quigley and learnt his name. He was in the class a year below me and was beginning his A-levels, but because he was in the IRA and I was holding an arms dump we had to be careful about our friendship. It wasn't until the guitar case with its arms and ammunition was removed in early 1971 that we could begin to go around together openly. However, almost immediately he disappeared from the scene, having been sentenced to six months in St Patrick's Boys' Home for possession of petrol bombs during a riot in Ballymurphy. Arrested with him, but sentenced to eighteen months in Belfast Prison, was Tom Hartley, whom I hadn't yet met.

Jimmy smoked but had little pocket money, and since I was working in a bar I could afford to buy him cigarettes, which I brought or sent up to him.

By the time he was released, internment had been introduced, and though I had moved on from his school to college we began socialising together and he often stayed in our house, especially after we had been to dances. I would throw a single mattress on the floor, parallel to my bed, for him to sleep on, though we spent most of the night talking away, into the early hours.

We usually tried to see home girlfriends who lived in the same street or vicinity, so that afterwards we would have each other for company as we made our way back to the house, or to my granny's house, which was up for sale after she moved to England and which I was minding. Most of my memories of him are associated with his beautiful smile and his infectious laugh. We had great adventures together and talked mainly of two subjects: love and politics.

On one occasion after a dance we persuaded two girls, Pauline and Eileen, to come and stay in my granny's.

'Of course there are beds in every room,' I lied.

They each told their parents they were staying in the other's house. They arrived with two teabags and no nightdresses. It was late October, below freezing, and we had no coal or electric fire. When they discovered there was only one double bed they accused me of being a 'dirty bastard' and took Jimmy under the sheets between them whilst I lay covered in a coat, shivering on the living-room floor. 'If only he had told the truth,' I heard Jimmy pronounce smugly to the two schoolgirls with no nightdresses.

The girls left at eight in the morning and Jimmy and I left for school and college. 'If only you had told the truth,' he laughed as we departed. A few days later, my mother, who occasionally checked my granny's, baffled me by asking what had happened to the Sacred Heart picture on the wall. I checked the house and it was true, it was gone, it had been stolen. When confronted, Eileen confessed that Pauline had put it up her coat on her way out. 'She said its eyes had followed her and that she had never seen one of those pictures before where God watches you as you go past.'

Jimmy and I investigated. We went to Pauline's house and confronted her but she denied having taken it. In the end, I had to go to the OC of the IRA in the Clonard area. He called to her house and demanded that she hand it back. She again denied having it. But her brother – who had been trying to get into the IRA – confirmed that he had seen a new Sacred Heart up on her bedroom wall. When she was out he stole the picture back – it was his first operation – and was accepted into the IRA.

I remounted the picture on the wall and then told my mother that when Jimmy and I were horsing around it fell from the wall and we had to take it to a shop to get the glass replaced, hence its absence for a time. I felt guilty when she gave me two pounds towards the cost of the repair.

Though I had held guns for the IRA and would, in a juvenile way, defend their actions against critics whom I thought offered no alternative, I had qualms about many aspects of IRA activity. I plagued Jimmy with various scenarios and asked him to convince me of the morality of this or that act. I think I used to exasperate him. One night in his house, when I was demanding answers (and, simultaneously, worrying that I might be undermining his convictions), he said, 'Danny, I volunteered to be led, not to lead.'

Jimmy was born in 1954, at home, in Cyprus Street. He had two older brothers, Roy and Frank. His father, Tommy, was a bread server, though later, when the other children were born, he supplemented his wages by working at night as a barman. After Jimmy, Mrs Quigley had Tommy, lost a girl when she was seven months pregnant (she slipped on linoleum and fell down the stairs), then had Gerard and Marcus. She was thirty-three when her last child, Brian, was just five weeks old and her husband died suddenly from a perforated ulcer.

Jimmy joined Na Fianna Éireann (a youth organisation linked to the more senior IRA) in 1967 or 1968, around the time that the movement for civil rights began in the North. It wasn't until a few years later, when soldiers raided the house and Frank and Jimmy escaped out the back window in their underwear, that Mrs Quigley realised they were both involved in the IRA. The area they lived in – a deprived, working-class area, a warren of cobblestoned streets running from the Falls Road and sloping down to Cullingtree Road – was steeped in republican history and had been the scene of conflict for over a hundred years.

When the area came under sustained attack by loyalists, B-Specials (a legal, Protestant paramilitary force) and the RUC in August 1969, the IRA was in a bad state and in no position to defend the area properly. The republican leadership in the preceding years had demilitarised much of the IRA and placed its hopes in constitutional reform, despite all the signs of hostility from the forces of the state and the unionist government. The lack of IRA readiness for a unionist backlash against the nationalist community contributed to a bitter split in the republican movement and the formation of the 'Provisional IRA'. Those who remained under the current leadership were referred to as the 'Officials'. Jimmy sided with the Provisionals, though he remained friends with many of his former comrades.

On 3 July 1970 British soldiers imposed a curfew in the Lower Falls and began raiding for arms, which until then had not been used against them, but were stored for use in the event of another loyalist attack. Both the Officials and the Provisionals fought the British army in gun battles while young people, like Jimmy's brothers Roy and Tommy, were out throwing stones at the invading soldiers. Jimmy spent that weekend moving weapons to safety, some of which, as I said earlier, he later brought to my house.

Tommy recalls the behaviour of the British army, which was to drive hundreds of young people, including himself, into the IRA.

'By the time it was getting dark, the shooting was really starting. A crowd of us were standing at a place called the Gap when a Saladin Tank wheeled around the corner. We couldn't believe it when it turned its cannon on us. We started running like lunatics and it fired.'

The soldiers had fired from the tank's 76mm main gun.

'The roar was deafening and the houses shook, but later we realised that they had fired a blank shell.'

Many people who were wounded or were suffering from the effects of inhaling CS gas were being treated in a local primary school, which had been turned into a first-aid station. Roy and Tommy were forced to retreat through the back streets, towards the centre of the area, and took refuge in the school.

'A ferret car pulled up outside the school and opened fire on the building with a machine-gun. The people were shouting out the windows, "This is a first-aid station! This is a first-aid station! There are people wounded in here!" The Brits got out and put an explosive device against the metal doors, which had been locked behind us, and blew them open. They stood pointing their rifles and shouted that if we came out and got searched they would let us go home. People started filing out, but when they got us outside they beat us up.

'We were put in the back of lorries and taken first to Springfield Road barracks, but it was packed with prisoners. Then to Andersonstown Barracks, but there was no room there, either. Finally, they took us over to Castlereagh Barracks in East Belfast.'

In custody, Tommy, who was fourteen, was assaulted. He and Roy were among over 240 people taken prisoner. Most were charged with riotous behaviour, but Roy and Tommy and over twenty others were remanded in custody charged with possession of a half-pound of explosives allegedly found in the school. Two weeks later they all got bail, and some months afterwards the charges were dropped.

From August 1971 onwards the Lower Falls became one of the IRA's strongest areas of support. The British army, when it raided, entered in armoured cars or in large numbers of foot patrols. Often the armoured cars would enter from the top of the district, on the Falls Road, and freewheel silently down through the streets to surprise IRA volunteers. Some of their vehicles were fitted with special silencers. These streets were regular battlegrounds where civilians, British soldiers and IRA volunteers lost their lives or suffered serious injuries.

Jimmy's mother, Mrs Quigley, recalls one incident when the British army raided the house opposite hers. The parents of the McLaughlin children were both dead, but the children, with the help of neighbours, were raising themselves. Mrs Quigley and another woman went over to remonstrate with the soldiers who were arresting twelve-year-old Martin. Unbeknownst to them, all the other neighbours had been told by the IRA to clear the street. The IRA then began throwing blast bombs at the troops.

The soldiers formally arrested Martin but Mrs Quigley insisted that she accompany him to the barracks. They were taken away in the back of a military jeep and held in the barracks for eight hours before being released without charge. When Mrs Quigley returned to her empty house (her younger sons having been sent to her mother's in the Whiterock area) she found 'the stairs downstairs' – they had been dislodged from the landing by one of the explosions – and the interior badly damaged. She had to move to Divis Flats, into a maisonette on Whitehall Row, which was derelict and filthy and which the family hated.

As 1971 came to a close Jimmy and I went to a New Year's Eve céilí in Clonard Hall. It was a great dance, but at the stroke of midnight many girls started crying because their boyfriends were in jail, and this put us in a sombre mood. Jimmy and I walked up the Falls Road to George's Shop, which stayed open all night, to get his cigarettes, then on the way back to my house we were stopped and searched by Scottish soldiers. At 3.30 AM I wrote in my diary, 'sitting talking, listening, communicating with Jimmy.'

He asked to write something in my diary and I handed it to him. He wrote:

I hereby declare that I, Jimmy Quigley, shall from this day forward, the first of January, read as many books, articles and writing as I possibly can. Dated, 1 January 1972.

I don't know how 1972 shall take me but I shall make this my year of years, and I hope I shall be able to say at the end of this year that I am satisfied with everything I have done, said, read and thought. I also hope that I will make the same resolution at the beginning of every year . . .

I shall make my mark on this earth and I hope I am worthy of this mark.

Your health! To my improvements and my ambitions. Up the Republic!

To which I added: 'YES'.

He called into our house on the night of Bloody Sunday. As we sat watching the television screens and pictures of the wounded and dying being carried away, I broke down and ran out of the room in tears, to everyone's embarrassment. My friends and I went out and rioted that night, providing cover for Jimmy and other IRA volunteers, who threw hand grenades at the soldiers.

By now, Jimmy's brother Frank was on the run. One day he was at an IRA meeting in a house when word arrived that soldiers were on foot patrol close by. He left immediately with an Armalite rifle to attack them but discovered that the soldiers had surrounded the area. He had to run through side streets and climb walls to get away. When he tried to leave the house in which he had taken refuge, he ran straight into a soldier, who pushed him back and began to search him. The soldier felt the rifle, pulled it out and began cheering to his mates. Frank kicked the soldier in the groin and then ran up the street. Local women were screaming for the soldiers not to shoot him. He was eventually cornered in a yard. His only chance of escape was to climb over a pigeon loft. But a soldier fired three shots at him. Frank threw himself into the next yard and tried to climb another wall but looked up and a soldier was pointing his gun at him.

'Right, I'm shooting you this time. You're dead this time,' the soldier said.

Frank shouted, 'Right! Right!' and was ordered to come back into the next yard. Two other soldiers had climbed onto the wall and Frank saw another opportunity. He began struggling with one of these soldiers for possession of his rifle when he was shot in the leg and fell. He was arrested and brought to an army barracks, where the soldiers wanted to interrogate him, but the doctor insisted he go to hospital. He was transferred to the military wing of Musgrave Hospital.

Shortly afterwards, Jimmy and Tommy were walking through the Lower Falls when soldiers shouted out through the slit in a Saracen armoured car, 'We got Quigley! We got Quigley!'

That night, I heard pebbles strike my window and looked out to discover that it was Jimmy, standing on a pile of bricks in next-door's yard. He was billeting in my neighbours' and asked me had I heard about Frank. The next day I went down to his house and, although Mrs Quigley was still in a state of shock, all the boys seemed excited – more relieved, probably – and quite proud of Frank.

The following Sunday, Jimmy and I went to a dance in Andersonstown and paired off with two sisters, whom we left home to Stewartstown Park, and then began our own long walk home. Jimmy said he was going to go to Divis Flats, instead of staying in our house. At he walked into the flats he was stopped by an army foot patrol, arrested and taken to Hollywood Barracks for interrogation.

A few days later Mrs Quigley received a telegram to say that Jimmy was detained (interned) on the *Maidstone* prison ship which was docked in Belfast Lough. He sent word out to me that during his interrogation he had been quizzed about my involvement in the IRA.

He wrote to Frank in Musgrave Hospital:

1 March 1972

I was lifted on Monday morning at 1 AM. They heard my name and recognised it from you. They took me to Hollywood where I did forty-eight hours wall-watching. Big Harry [O'Rawe] and his cousin, Rickie, are here and Harry says that he has had millions of girls writing to him . . .

I got a visit from Mammy today. She took it bad as usual. If you can write, keep it clean [secure]. The warders are decent but the Queen's Own Highlanders can usually force themselves to say a few nasty words . . .

He also wrote to Frank's wife, Josie:

I jumped with joy when I got your letter . . . Tell all the girls not to worry – I won't be long in here, ha, ha! Josie, as I wrote that line I received another letter. Hold on! I've just received another! It's funny, they were both from girls.

I cannot think of anything else to say, so while I am thinking I will crack the old *Maidstone* joke. We are, at this moment, cruising on the Caribbean Sea. I am surrounded by beautiful girls, as much drink as anyone can hold, and all the beautiful music of the world. Or, if you like – wine, women and song!

I am getting a beautiful suntan, with special suntan lotion put on by a British soldier. And I don't like it very much because he uses a large lump of wood (I think they call it a baton!).

Three weeks later he wrote to Frank:

Chris Clarke [his cousin] was up to see me on Saturday. She kissed me goodbye. The first sex I've had in weeks! It meant a lot but don't tell her that! My 'Ma' was up today (that is just to attack you for writing 'mother'). She was telling me that you threw your arms around her and kissed her. She was as pleased as punch. It must have made her day, month, year, her life, worthwhile! You big slob!

Our faithful little brother Tommy – the hard-hitting, hard-drinking, hard-swearing man, who could have his fill of all the girls in the country – hasn't written me a letter yet. Josie and Vera [Josie's sister] wrote to me. Josie wrote twice . . .

I have an idea and if you don't like it tell me to piss off. This is it. While you are there why don't you try to educate yourself and when you get out you might be able to take some exams and get a good job. Well, it's only an idea.

Look after yourself and keep the chin up.

Mrs Quigley was working in a chip shop in the flats when her son Brian came down and said, 'Mammy, there's a man upstairs and he wants to see you.' She said, 'Who is it?' but he wouldn't tell her. 'I went up and it was Jimmy. Then he went up to see you, Danny, in Paddy Hynes' pub.'

Two weeks before Jimmy's release, the British government prorogued the Stormont Parliament and suspended unionist rule. A Secretary of State, William Whitelaw, was appointed to take control of affairs, and one of his initiatives was to begin reviewing internees' cases.

I was sitting drinking with some other republicans in our local bar, Hynes', when Jimmy walked in and surprised us. He was given a great cheer and responded with that beautiful smile of his. Immediately, we organised a party, which continued in his Whitehall Row flat until the early hours.

Two days later he was back on active service.

Meanwhile, Frank had been charged with possession of a rifle with intent to endanger life. In the shooting his leg had been badly damaged and the nerves to his foot severed. He was operated on, sent to Crumlin Road Jail, then returned to Musgrave Hospital to be fitted with a calliper. One day Mrs

Quigley phoned Musgrave to find out if Frank was still there or if he had been transferred back to Crumlin Road.

The soldier who took the call said to her, 'You're awful fucking funny', and slammed down the phone. As Mrs Quigley and her sister Kathleen walked up the Falls Road, everybody was winking at them and smiling.

'I came back to the flat. Jimmy was sitting doing some homework. Brian, Marcus and Gerard were sitting on the floor, watching the television. I said to Jimmy that I was arranging a visit with Frank but that they were awfully ignorant with me. Jimmy laughed. "You'll have to go to the Free State to see Frank. He's escaped!" It had already been on the news, but I didn't know.'

Frank had become friendly with several soldiers who were guarding the prisoners, about eight in all, most of whom were civilians shot by the British Army or the RUC and facing prosecution on trumped-up charges. Another prisoner was twenty-two-year-old IRA volunteer Jim Mulvenna from North Belfast, who had, miraculously, survived being shot nine times a few weeks earlier.

Frank befriended a British army captain who one day said that if he were to escape, he would not go out through the front, as that would be 'a waste of time. Go out that way, you're dead. They'll shoot you. The best way is to cut through the bars. It's easy. It's not a problem. That's the way I would go.'

Hacksaw blades were smuggled in inside the nappy of Frank's son, Cormac.

Only Jim Mulvenna was interested in the escape. There was a window covered by long drapes beside his bed in the ward. 'We decided to cut our way through the bars,' said Frank. It took longer than expected, and to mask the noise of the sawing the other prisoners would sing loudly or shout and cheer.

After the killing of two soldiers by snipers in Derry, the chief medical officer approached Frank, as leader of the prisoners. He complained about the singing. 'Have we not treated you very well? Treated you like soldiers?'

Frank agreed that they had.

'Well, after two of our men were killed last night there was a lot of singing and cheering, which has made our men very angry.'

Frank said that they were only trying to keep their spirits up. 'It's not like that at all. Tell your men we are sorry but we were not cheering at anybody getting killed.'

Two nights later the bars were cut, but then they had to saw through the window frame. On the night of the escape, Frank and Jim Mulvenna fashioned bed sheets into a rope. They dropped to the ground from the second-storey window. Jim was in pyjamas and Frank had his own clothes but no shoes. They made their way through the grounds, hid in bushes, then, by climbing a tree, made their way over the perimeter fence and onto the main road. Jim was very weak and fell a number of times. Frank left him hidden in the garden of a house and went to get support. They had had lifts arranged for previous nights, but their helpers had given up and presumed that the escape was abandoned. It took Frank several hours to get in contact with West Belfast, and by that time Jim, thinking he had been caught or trapped, had tried to make his way to the Falls Road.

It is possible that someone seeing a man dressed in pyjamas and walking along the M1 reported it to the RUC. Jim was arrested in Milltown Cemetery. He was later sentenced to four years in jail. Two years after his release he was on active service with William Mailey and Dinny Brown when the three unarmed men were surrounded by the SAS and shot dead.

Frank went across the border, recovered, got fitted with a special calliper in Dublin, and returned to active service in Belfast around June 1972.

Tommy Quigley left school in 1971 and worked for a wholesale pharmacist in Northumberland Street, between the Falls and

Shankill, but he was sacked for taking a day off to attend a rally protesting against Bloody Sunday. Four weeks before Frank's return to Belfast, Tommy and three others were arrested carrying out an armed robbery and charged with attempted murder (shots were fired at an RUC man when they were surrounded, and another plain-clothes RUC man had been held hostage). Throughout the summer of 1972 he was held on remand in Crumlin Road Jail.

Jimmy stayed in houses around the Beechmount area, using false identity papers which helped him avoid arrest. But he became restless and he and I had cross words a number of times, though looking back I haven't a clue over what. He talked increasingly about moving down to D Company, to join Frank, and I think I resented this and took it as some sort of slight on our friendship. Nevertheless, after he left we remained the best of friends, and when we saw each other we caught up on all our gossip and speculated on the way we saw things going.

I saw him early one morning in late September 1972, a few days after I returned from England. I told him I had a new girl and he told me he was going out with someone. Whatever we had to say to each other, we were both laughing, and when we parted, he shouted after me, 'If only you had told the truth!'

Tommy can't remember where he was in the jail when he heard that someone had been shot in the Lower Falls district. Jimmy was due up on a visit and would have all the information. As he was waiting to be called, he sat in a cell chatting to some friends, when his OC came in and asked everyone but Tommy to leave. He then told Tommy that Frank had been shot dead.

'I was numb. He left and I broke down. The lads came back to the cell and tried to console me. Then I got called for my visit and I went to the toilets to wash my face, which was pure red from crying.'

Tommy's cousin, Chrissie Clarke, who was seventeen, was working in a city-centre clothes shop that lunchtime when one of her co-workers said that a boy called Quigley had been killed in a shooting.

'I started crying and ran upstairs to the storeroom. My sister Betty was shopping that day, along with her child, and called in. She said there were many people of that name and it mightn't be our cousin. I was still upset and so Betty said she would take me home. As we walked along Castle Street to get a taxi, we met a man who said he knew the father of the lad who had just been killed, so that ruled out any of our cousins because their daddy, Tommy, had been dead for years. Betty said, "See. It's somebody else." But I still wanted to go home.'

Frank's wife, Josie, was visiting her mother in Ballymurphy that day. 'Word came up that somebody had been shot dead down the Falls and that his name was Quigley. I thought right away it was Frank and rushed to try and get back down the road. I can't remember exactly what happened. There were gun battles raging and I searched for Frank's mother, Mary, but couldn't find her.'

Earlier that day, Friday 29 September 1972, Mrs Quigley had been taken shopping by Jimmy, who had just received a cheque for seventy pounds as part of a school grant. 'He bought me a fur coat in Sinclair's, and he got himself a new sports coat, shoes and shirt. We called in to Sawyers' and bought a load of white fish and cream buns because we were in the money! He left me at a quarter to eleven and I got the bus in Castle Street to go up to my hairdresser's, Janet Farrell, to get my hair done for the weekend.'

Mrs Quigley's fifteen-year-old son, Gerard, was walking up Albert Street when the shooting started, and he ran towards Raglan

Street. He saw the soldiers who carried out the shooting from a balcony in Divis Flats. He remembers there being a bomb scare on the Falls Road at the scene of the funeral of a Catholic man killed in a loyalist explosion, and seeing an armoured car sitting at the corner of McDonnell Street. He also saw a body – the person who had been shot – hanging out of an attic window on the third floor, above Caulfield's chemist shop, but he could not recognise who it was.

Mary McConville's maternal uncle, Seamus 'Rocky' Burns, was a Belfast IRA Volunteer who had been killed in a gun battle with the RUC in June 1944. Mary's mother, Madge, was imprisoned in the forties and was again to be interned without trial in Armagh prison in 1973 when she was a grandmother. Mary had joined the republican youth organisation for girls, Cumann na gCailíní, in 1968, and later was imprisoned on a number of occasions. She had known Jimmy for four years, from when na gCailíní and na Fianna trained together. That day, she had just left work and gone home for lunch when she heard shooting.

'I ran up Albert Street and saw a body lying out of an attic window. There had been shooting and a large crowd had gathered. The soldiers were pushing and shoving and there was a lot of screaming and shouting. There's a lot about that day is hazy, but I remember the Brits throwing the body into a Saracen and I got up close and I thought it was Frankie Quigley.'

Shortly after the shooting, Gerard Quigley found his nineteen-year-old brother Frank. Frank told him what information he had – Jimmy had been wounded – and to go and find their mother and let her know.

Mary McConville, who at first thought the body was that of Frank, realised it was Jimmy after she got a closer look and before she was pushed away by the soldiers.

Mrs Quigley cannot remember Gerard coming into the hairdresser's and thinks it was Marcus, who would then have been fourteen. 'I was under the dryer when Marcus came in with another lad and said that he'd been told that Jimmy had been shot in the hand.'

When Chrissie Clarke arrived home, her father, Chris (Mrs Quigley's older brother and something of a guardian to her sons), told her that one of the Quigley boys had been up to say that Jimmy had been wounded but he was all right.

Janet Farrell closed up the hairdresser's immediately and accompanied Mrs Quigley to the Royal Victoria Hospital. 'It's all a mist now,' recalled Mrs Quigley. 'We got to the hospital and made inquiries. A sister came out and she wanted me to "identify" Jimmy. I thought he had been shot in the hand and I couldn't understand. I just couldn't go in. Janet went in. She came out and nodded to me that it was Jimmy. She said that there was a coloured soldier lying beside him . . . I can't remember coming out of the hospital. When we came over to the Falls there were gun battles and we couldn't get home.'

In Crumlin Road Jail, as Tommy Quigley stood washing his face, his friend and co-accused, Toby McMahon, came and said, 'Tommy, it's not Frankie. I don't think it's Frankie . . . '

Tommy recalls that for a fraction of a second he was overwhelmed with relief before hearing Toby say, 'I think it's Jimmy.'

When Tommy went out to the visiting box, his cousin Chrissie was waiting with the news. 'She was trying to tell me what exactly happened to Jimmy but it was all a blur.'

I was downtown, sitting in Kieran Meehan's car while he was signing on for the dole. He came back to the car and said, 'Somebody told me they heard that the fella shot dead was Quigley from the Flats.' As we came up Divis Street, I stopped a member of the Official IRA, who told me that it was Jimmy who had been killed. My stomach turned and I felt sick. I asked Kieran to bring me home. The house was empty.

I went up to the bedroom where he and I had lain for hours talking and laughing and arguing and I lay down and cried convulsively. When I heard my sister Susan and Mammy come in, I rushed down to tell them. Susan and Jimmy had gone out a few times together earlier that year and Susan burst into tears.

Mrs Quigley eventually got back to her flat. It was full of friends and relatives preparing the house for the wake.

'But then the soldiers wouldn't let Jimmy out of the hospital. They said he hadn't been formally identified so we had to get my brother Chris to go over and identify him again. My mother had died four days earlier and we had just buried her. We buried her on one Tuesday and Jimmy on the following Tuesday . . . '

When the remains came home the coffin was draped in a tricolour and the IRA provided a guard of honour. The only entrance and exit to Quigley's flat could be observed from the British army billet at the top of Divis Tower, and during the wake there was a heavy presence of soldiers on the landings. They stopped and searched mourners. At one point the soldiers attempted to raid the wake, possibly looking for Frank, who was on the run. Chrissie pleaded with the soldiers at the front door: 'Our Jimmy's in there. Please give us a break,' she said. But she was pushed aside and there was a fight on the stairs.

Tommy applied for compassionate bail to attend the funeral but the high court judge dismissed his application in minutes.

At Jimmy's funeral four IRA Volunteers using AR18s came to attention fired a volley of shots over the coffin when it stopped in Leeson Street. A careful look at the photograph which captures this moment, and which was published in much of the press, shows that one of the Volunteers is out of formation. He has a stiff leg.

Frank was the quartermaster of D Company and had given Jimmy the Garand rifle he had asked for. Jimmy, who was almost six feet tall, put the muzzle down one leg of his trousers and tucked the butt under his armpit and covered it with his jacket.

Frank's wife Josie was opening her door in Plevna Street when she saw Jimmy going down Osman Street.

'He waved to me and I waved back and he shouted, "I'll be in later." He was limping and I remember thinking, "Christ, Jimmy's got a sore leg. Sure I'll ask him when he comes in what happened his leg." It wasn't until afterwards,' said Josie, 'that I realised that Jimmy was limping because he was carrying and hiding his rifle. He was on his way when I saw him.'

Jimmy had planned to ambush a patrol coming out of Divis Flats. He had chosen a second-floor derelict attic above Caulfield's chemist's shop at the junction of Albert Street and McDonnell Street as his firing position. He was accompanied by a seventeen-year-old youth who himself had been seriously wounded by British soldiers some months earlier and was still recovering. He carried a .45 Webley revolver.

'We were up in the attic about ten or fifteen minutes and a couple of times Jimmy changed position to have a look out of the window,' he said. 'I was sitting at the back of the room. Jimmy was watching the flats opposite, and the road, then he said, "They're out of their Saracen!"'

'I said, "Can you see any, can you take a shot?"'

'He looked out and said, "Hold on, hold on."'

'We then heard noises and only afterwards did I learn that they were actually beneath us. I said, "Fuck! What's that?"'

'He said, "Look out the back window and see if you can see anything."'

'I left him and went to the back and pulled open a piece of corrugated iron. I put my head out and a soldier, who was on the flat roof, put a rifle to my head. I was expecting to be whacked at any second. I shouted, "British army! What are youse after! What are youse after! I'm only collecting lead!", hoping to alert Jimmy. There was another soldier, a black soldier, on the roof as well. The soldier pointing his gun at me said, "Get out on the roof! Get out on the roof!"

'I still had the Webley in my belt and he shouted, "Search! Search!" for me to open my coat. All of a sudden we heard four large bangs, shots being fired. I think that was when Jimmy was hit. Nothing happened but then, within sixty seconds – it could have been longer, it could have been shorter – there were more shots and the other soldier, the black soldier, had looked out to see what was happening and was shot dead.

'The soldier who had been guarding me suddenly took off. I couldn't believe it. I then escaped across the walls, in through a house, out the front and through a crowd of people rushing up the next street.'

The soldier killed was eighteen-year-old Ian Burt from the Royal Anglian Regiment. He had been shot by an IRA sniper firing from Bosnia Street.

A rumour swept the Lower Falls that the raiding party had desecrated Jimmy's body and thrown it from the window to the ground, and this fuelled the anger of local people and sparked off widespread rioting. Later that day, in the same area, the British army shot dead twenty-year-old Patricia McKay, a member of the Official IRA, who was unarmed at the time of her death.

In October 1972 Tommy was sentenced to five years in jail.

Frank was recaptured in September 1973. He was one of the first people sentenced under the new Diplock Court system, which sat without a jury. Some of the witnesses had since left the British army. The soldier who shot him in the leg gave conflicting evidence. Another former soldier, this time in handcuffs, having himself become a prisoner in the meantime, told the court, 'That's definitely not the gunman.'

Frank had no lawyer and didn't speak. The judge, Lord Chief Justice Sir Robert Lowry (nephew of Robert Lynd), sentenced him to three years in jail.

In December 1972, Chrissie Clarke, aged seventeen, was sentenced to four years for possession of a revolver.

Frank was released and reported back to the IRA. In 1982 he was arrested in County Louth, close to the South Armagh border, and charged with possession of explosives and firearms. He was sentenced to eight years in jail.

After his release Tommy also reported back to the IRA. In 1983 he was arrested and sentenced to life imprisonment, with a recommendation that he serve at least thirty-five years for a series of bombings in England during the 1981 hunger strike. He served over fifteen years of his sentence and was released under the terms of the Belfast Agreement.

Over a twenty-nine-year period, from 1970 until 1999, Mrs Quigley visited her sons in jail.

'Jimmy was always very quiet, always studying, always had his head stuck in a book,' recalls Mrs Quigley. 'In his exams he always came eighth out of a class of thirty-two. I used to encourage him and say, "That's good," but he replied, "No, I should be further up than that. I want to be first or second."

'Frank always seemed to slide through everything but Jimmy had to work awfully hard at it. He was doing an exam one time and I said to him, "Pray to St Joseph of Cupertino." He said, "Who's he?" I said, "He's a wee boy who lived in Germany and there was a statue of Our Lady in the square. He used to go over and pray to Our Lady to help him pass his exams. But he failed his exams and afterwards lifted a stone and hit the statue on the face and the blood ran down the statue's face. So she came to him in a dream that night and said to him, 'I have other things for you, you don't need to pass any exams', and he died a fortnight later." Jimmy says, "I'm not praying to him!"'

In 1971 Jimmy had been Frank's best man at his wedding to Josie McLaughlin and later was godfather to their child, Cormac.

'He loved being an uncle at just seventeen,' said Josie. 'He used to call in and say, "Put the child's hat on, Josie, and I'll take him out." You have to remember, this was thirty years ago when no lad, no man, would have carried a child; they were too macho. He would take Cormac over to his mammy's in the flats.'

Josie remembers Jimmy coming into her small kitchen when she was baking buns and lending a hand. 'We were like the Craddocks on the TV cookery show. We'd take the buns out of the oven and sit down to taste our own cooking. "Aren't they beautiful, Fanny?" he would say. "Just gorgeous, Johnny," I would reply, then we'd burst out laughing.'

A year after Jimmy's death Mrs Quigley left Whitehall Row. 'The soldiers had me tortured. They raided constantly, looking for Frank. I was working in a chip shop, sometimes from four until two in the morning, and would come home exhausted. I would wake up and there would be a soldier standing over me with a gun in my face. They used to sit on the sofa for hours on end. One soldier sat and told me his life story. He himself had a wee boy of about twelve. He got leave early on one occasion and went home to find his wife in bed with another man and that wrecked his life.

'There was a Major Alex who raided regularly. I said to him, "Do you really think my Frank would come here, knowing that you are all around here." He said: "He has to come and see his mother some time."

'And he did.'

Two months after Jimmy's death, I was interned. His mother, despite all that was on her plate, visited and wrote to me. Most of my letters were destroyed in jail but I copied one of hers into my diary. On 29 November 1973, she wrote:

> I suppose you think I have forgotten all about you; well I haven't. I think about you very often and remember when you came every Thursday night with forty Embassy for Jimmy . . . every time I think of Jimmy I think of you . . .
>
> A little boy was killed outside my door on Saturday night [a reference to seventeen-year-old Michael Marley, shot dead by the British Army] and I have been thinking of you both ever since. Danny, don't think talking about Jimmy will annoy me, not from you it won't.
>
> . . . a few weeks ago in your house, and your mother and I went up to Hynes' [bar]. Your father was there, and Danny, Jimmy would have laughed: we went to the same dance and we know the same people and we talked about them and how they were doing now we are all older people. But we were very young then and we did not have the life

that the young people have now with soldiers and internment camps and being locked up like animals . . . please forgive me, I did not mean to depress you . . .

Goodnight, son, God bless, and send you home soon. All my love,

Mary

From the *Irish News*, 14 December 1973:

INQUESTS

Open verdicts were also returned on a young married woman and a seventeen-year-old youth shot dead by soldiers in separate incidents during an eleven-hour gun battle in the Lower Falls in September last year.

The first to die was James Quigley, of Whitehall Row, Divis Flats, said to have been seen with a rifle at an attic window in Albert Street by soldiers guarding a bomb-disposal team.

The inquest was told that other soldiers went to the shop and Quigley climbed out the attic window and tried to escape over the roof. Soldiers watching him from Divis Flats fired a number of shots at him and he was killed instantly.

He fell back down the roof and landed on top of his rifle. The body and rifle were both recovered by soldiers. A soldier guarding the recovery party was shot in the head by a sniper and died a short time later.

A police inspector told the court that Quigley was described in death notices in a Belfast morning paper as a member of the Provisional IRA and it was stated that he had 'died on duty'.

Quigley's death, the inspector said, occurred at 1 PM on 29 September last year and sparked off a gun battle which lasted until midnight.

Jimmy had been going out with a girl, herself an activist and on the run at the time of his death. She is now married and has two children, a son of nineteen and a daughter of fifteen.

Jimmy's death shattered me. In jail, a few months later, he came to me in a wonderful dream, bursting with happiness and laughing. I knew him for a mere two years and can only explain my great sense of loss by the fondness and love his personality generated in those around him.

Often I think of him in relation to the thousands of things I have done since 1972; the pleasures he has missed – fatherhood, relationships; the music he would have loved; the life he would have led. There is not a day I do not think about him. He can never leave me.

'When people talk about closure I don't know what that really means,' said Tommy. 'I don't think there's a point in time when you are healed from it. It is still a raw wound and always will be. There's never been a sense of a "normal" mourning process . . . It has no ending.'

I spoke to Mrs Quigley when I came to write this. She said, 'I often wonder what Jimmy would have ended up working at, how things would have been, if the Troubles hadn't come along.'

'It's hard to believe that it is thirty years ago,' I said to her.

'Jimmy's forty-eight this year,' she whispered.

INTO THE CORE

In an entry in my diary for 15 December 1970, three weeks before my eighteenth birthday, I report having had a long conversation with Neil McCartney in the Falls Library. Neil was an alcoholic, a wino in his late fifties or older, who had, a few years before, begun drinking methylated spirits which he 'cut' with milk, in order to escape from this world.

The whites of Neil's eyes were actually turning methylated blue. At nights he stayed in Divis Street's Morning Star hostel, where I occasionally worked for the Legion of Mary.

Neil McCartney was a grizzly, tough, ill-tempered man, who intimidated other residents with a growl. He despised life and didn't like anyone to get close to him. But he befriended me and I encouraged him to talk. He left the hostel after breakfast each morning and walked considerable distances to get his hands on meths, as no one on the road would sell him it. He returned to West Belfast in the afternoon, rested, sometimes dozed in the Falls Library, furtively sipping his little bottle, before returning to the hostel for his dinner and bed. I met and sat with him many times in the library. On 19 January 1971 I wrote in my diary: 'He [Neil] spoke wisdom and truth of life and he hinted I think that any small thing can sometimes reduce a man and ruin his life.'

I learnt that he had taken part in the Spanish Civil War in support of Franco. Later, he fell in love with and married an English girl. He worked as a train driver or engineer. He and his wife lived in London but when war broke out he served in the British army as a sergeant. He came home on leave one day to find that his wife had been killed during the Blitz.

Understandably, Neil could never get his life back together but had, incredibly, survived the slide into alcoholism for another twenty-five years. A few months later Neil stopped drinking and told me he was trying to get a flat, but it was too late. He had a stroke, could no longer walk, and was transferred to a nursing home in Whiteabbey in grounds which overlooked Belfast Lough. I visited him once. They wheeled him out into the garden but I could get no sense out of him. The roses were in bloom, the bees buzzing. When I left him I was going for a glass of beer. After my exams I was planning to hitch-hike around Ireland. Neil sat in his chair staring into space, occasionally conscious of my presence, and now and again showed a conspiratorial smile. He died a short time later.

The previous December, when we sat together in the library, we talked about everything under the sun and he quizzed me about my life. I went home and wrote in my diary:

'You may not believe this but I have been endowed with patience. The proof of this lies in years from now of which I am part.

'A MAN is Cornelius Columbus McCartney.

'He made a prediction for me. A WRITER.'

But so incredible was the idea that I hadn't the nerve to write 'writer' and filled in only one line from each letter of the word, though it is discernible what the full word is. Later, I wrote, 'TAKE NOTE, "Into the Core"', which was the secret, notional title

I had for my first novel and which was meant to act as early proof of my intentions when I would look back.

On 17 January 1971 I wrote: 'I will now state that my aim is to write. Now we will see if that happens. The years, toil, trouble, sweat, heartaches – the years to come, more of this plus – read on to find out.' In April I bought a typewriter, but the first thing I wrote on it which was published was a letter to the *Irish News* protesting against the behaviour of the British army.

I might have become the writer of *Into the Core* – and a different writer from the one that I am – had the Troubles not come along and had I not made the choices I did.

My mother, who loved to read, introduced me to the extra-curricular world of books. Being kept busy looking after four children, a home and a husband, it was me she sent to the public library on Slievegallion Drive. 'Anything by Catherine Cookson or Victoria Holt,' she said to me. 'Or Catherine Marchant or Jean Plaidy.' I didn't know that Marchant was another name used by Cookson, and Plaidy a name used by Holt, but I got to know romances by their covers, ex-perimented with other authors and never brought her the same book twice.

I too joined the library and began reading children's books, mostly Enid Blyton's 'Famous Five' and 'Secret Seven' series. Inspired by their adventures my friend Brendan Hunter and I would follow suspicious strangers or potential great train robbers and write down our observations about their move-ments in little notebooks. We would lie out on Brendan's front lawn on summer nights, staring up at the stars, and make up stories about the people we followed.

I was never into Biggles, juvenile fiction's greatest flying hero, James Bigglesworth, or war stories, though later I loved John Buchan's 'Richard Hannay' series, and read all of Ian Fleming, Dennis Wheatley and, my favourite, Graham Greene. However, I saw reading as a hobby, like swimming, not a passion or a preparation for some vocation.

I liked being asked by my teacher, Mr Sands, to read aloud in the classroom, and enjoyed English homework. My favourite book at primary school was Rosemary Sutcliffe's *Simon*. Simon was a Cromwellian soldier during the Eng lish civil war whose best friend is a Royalist. The story is about loyalty and friendship. I haven't seen that book in over forty years yet can vividly recall one of the characters, perhaps because of his eccentric name: Pentecost Fiddler.

Joe Magee sat next to me in class. Joe always had plenty of pocket money and at his behest I produced a couple of hand-drawn-and-hand-written comics, for which he paid handsomely. Each edition had to include a story in which Joe was the hero who saved the world.

When I was twelve, we in our street had a gang, though that word conjures up the wrong impression, given that we were completely innocent souls. Stephen was about nine years of age, had red hair and lots of freckles and was about our most timid member. We dandered to the pictures to see *The Great Escape* but afterwards marched from the cinema together, with our chests out, and went back another two or three times. Stephen lived a few doors below me in Iveagh Parade. We had guiders (go-karts) which we or our fathers built. Stephen, who was an only child, was playing on his guider when another neighbour, reversing a minibus, accidentally struck him. I don't think his injuries were serious but it was while he was in hospital that it was discovered he had leukaemia. We rarely saw Stephen when he was allowed home and he died not long after.

It was raining on the day of his funeral and we, his friends in the gang, walked up the Falls Road in a bewildered state behind the hearse. After the burial I went to my bedroom, and using some of the words of the McCartney/Lennon song 'Yesterday', which was then in the charts, wrote down my feelings in an exercise book.

I am sure there were too many reminders of Stephen in our street for his parents to cope with – our faces and laughter to begin with; our growing up; the corner itself, where Stephen was struck. His parents moved away and I can't remember hearing about them until just a few years ago when I met a woman, a relation of theirs. She told me that Stephen's mother and father had gone on to have another child. She was also able to tell me that I had written a piece about Stephen, and it was only then that I remembered the details. My mother must have found what I had written and shown or given it to Stephen's grandmother.

When I was fourteen I kept a small notebook in my back pocket and occasionally wrote down personal thoughts, usually about girls that I liked. On one occasion while playing handball with my friend Jimmy Boner (who was shot dead in 1972, a few months before his father was killed), the notebook fell from my pocket and he quickly picked it up. I made the mistake of panicking and Jimmy held the notebook at arm's length. I had to give him thruppence to return it without reading it!

It wasn't until 1968 that I began keeping small diaries and then, later, larger ones.

At the end of my diary for 1968 I have written in a section under NOTES FOR 1969 that by that July I should have left Glen Road Christian Brothers School, and by September 1969 'I should be working now at electronic engineering.' As a child I had wanted to be a veterinary surgeon, then a draughtsman, before becoming interested in building radios and transmitters. Instead, by September 1969 I had moved to St Mary's Grammar School to study A-level mathematics, physics, and economic and political science (which we jokingly called ESP – extra sensory perception – and which I hated. Politics!).

I didn't know what I would be doing at university with those subjects or what career I would opt for, but the circumstances never arose. Firstly, although I enjoyed pure maths, particularly resolving algebraic equations, I couldn't really concentrate on my studies because I was still madly in love with Angela, whom I had been introduced to in August. She was a friend of Rosemary, who went with my friend Tony. One night, to my delight, he asked me to make up a foursome. I remember seeing her standing beneath a tree on the Falls Road, when the trees were still in leaf, before they were felled for barricades.

Fifteen years of age, long fair hair, the reward of the loveliest smile on her assumption that the tangle of your eyes with hers was innocent. The magic of innocently beholding her. A party in Tony's house, which one of his big sisters was supposed to have organised, had been cancelled, but we went into his parlour anyway, paired off, played records – the Stones and the Beatles – and put out the lights.

Kissing Angela was like floating in the sweetest dream.

And then I blew it. Lying on the sofa, her blouse had come partially undone. Suddenly, my fingers were running over her stomach and the sensation for me was electric. Infused with passion, at the sexual peak of my life, I decided to explore further and moved my hand across her bra. When she rebuffed me with her arm, in no uncertain terms, I died with shame at my foolhardiness. We still kissed but her feeling for me had withered.

The following day I told Rosemary to tell her I was sorry.

And so, for months afterwards, I would dream about her, though there were nights when I couldn't sleep and days when I couldn't eat or think straight. I would go out of my way to cross her path coming out of Mass or going to school. Each day when I passed Tony's house my heart would force my eyes to seek out the window of his parlour and to recall and relish that night.

I found out that Angela was besotted with another friend of mine, which made my heart ache even more. It was around this time that I found a new solace in fiction and was rewarded, ironically, by a sweet sadness, by feelings of melancholy. In school, when I should have been studying course work, I spent my time in the studies hall pensively reading books like

Wuthering Heights. I found myself at one with Heathcliff's obsession with Cathy:

> . . . for what is not connected with her to me? And what does not recall her? I cannot look down to this floor, but her features are shaped on the flags! In every cloud, in every tree – filling the air at night, and caught by glimpses in every object, by day I am surrounded with her image! . . . The entire world is a dreadful collection of memoranda that she did exist, and that I have lost her!

My obsession with Angela lasted about two years, and though we eventually became good friends, and I loved being in her company, we never spoke about that night. I even dated her younger sister once, perversely trying but failing to recreate the alchemy, as if such magic could run in a family. Around 1972 we disappeared from each other's lives. She later happily married a mutual friend, going on to have three children, and moved to the countryside.

I fell behind in my work – which I had lost interest in, anyway, given that I was studying the wrong subjects; left St Mary's school and went to St Peter's Secondary to study English literature and maths, but, again, skipped classes and sneaked off to an empty room to read D. H. Lawrence or Virginia Woolf. I left St Peter's and went to the College of Business Studies to study English and history, but left without completing the course, having joined the republican movement full-time.

It was to be thirty years before I was back in the classrooms of Glen Road CBS and St Mary's, and then it was to address the English literature classes on creative writing and the short story.

Reading literature was a liberating, transcendent and cathartic experience, allowing one to go beyond the sciences, to enter into the private minds of other souls – into the core – to understand motivation, to empathise with characters in their conflicts with life. Henry Miller described the frisson he experienced when as a child he started to read fiction and discovered character: 'They were alive and they spoke to me!' Or, as Jerzi Kosinski's unnamed hero in *The Painted Bird* observed: 'In ordinary life . . . one saw many people without really knowing them, while in books one even knew what people were thinking and planning.'

Characters haunted me, accompanied me. I went out with a girl called Ena but thought of her as Millie from Michael Farrell's *Thy Tears Might Cease*.

I felt I was a 'comedian' straight out of the book of that title by Graham Greene.

I cried when Chief Bromden smothered the lobotomised Randall Patrick McMurphy with a pillow to put him out of his misery, before the chief escaped from the mental institution.

I felt the death of Michael Henchard and read his will with tears in my eyes:

> that no sexton be asked to toll the bell.
> & that nobody is wished to see my dead body.
> & that no murners walk behind me at my funeral.
> & that no flours be planted on my grave.
> & that no man remember me.

I sobbed with the elderly Lucy Smalley as she sat on the toilet, addressing her husband, retired Colonel 'Tusker' Smalley, who had just died and left her 'staying on', alone and stranded in post-colonial India.

And I return again and again to my favourite book, *Knulp* by Hermann Hesse, for its simplicity and spirituality, because it speaks to me and offers meaning.

Knulp is a vagrant but he has many friends in many towns. He whistles, sings, and reads poetry. He is fortyish and dying of consumption, but something draws him back to his old village. When he returns, nothing is the same. In his youth he gave up a promising scholarly career for a girl, who then was unfaithful, and this changed the course of his life. In his last days he wanders up the mountain and is cursing his fate when God suddenly appears. God explains to Knulp that it had been the whole purpose of Knulp's life to bring a little nostalgia for freedom into the lives of others, to make the children laugh and the people dance.

> 'So you've nothing more to complain about?' God's voice asked.
>> 'Nothing more,' Knulp nodded with a shy laugh.
>> 'And everything's all right? Everything is as it should be?'
>> 'Yes,' he nodded. 'Everything is as it should be.'

And after the last sentence on the last page I simply sigh and swallow hard.

While interned in Long Kesh I eventually sat A-level English literature and scraped through with a grade 'C'. That was my highest formal educational achievement until I was awarded a distinction in the Open University's Arts Foundation Course in 1992, while in jail serving an eight-year sentence.

In 1975, during an IRA ceasefire, at twenty-two I became editor of *Republican News,* and, in 1979, editor of *An Phoblacht/ Republican News* when the party's two papers merged. I had also been national director of publicity for many years prior to my arrest in 1990.

The reason I hesitated to write fiction – even part-time, while I was involved in the republican movement – was that I lacked confidence and had lost my earlier instincts. I felt I needed much more reading experience than I had. I also had a romantic view of writers as being a mix of angst-ridden, bohemian, eccentric, iconoclastic individuals, great drinkers and lovers, outside of society, a law unto themselves, mad and peculiar; whereas I had a fundamentalist disposition and was entrenched in a movement, a struggle and a propaganda war in which words were weapons and language was finely calibrated.

Nevertheless, in 1986 I decided to write a novel and began gathering notes and ideas. I wrote in my spare time and usually into the early hours of the morning. I told no one until it was two-thirds complete, for fear of being ridiculed. But my motives for writing were twofold. Firstly, I wanted to see if I could write, if I could people a long piece of prose with credible characters whose lives were interesting. Secondly, my subject matter was material with which I was intimately familiar: how a section of the nationalist community in the 1960s and early 1970s could move from a position of relative pacifism to one of support for IRA activity.

West Belfast was published in late 1989, a few weeks before I was arrested and imprisoned. It is about the loss of innocence at both the individual and community level. It was popular with republicans and their supporters, and with those who could empathise with the alienated and marginalised, but was savaged by many reviewers, some of whom merely concentrated on the sniper scene or accused me of flaunting 'the sexuality of violence'. Not surprisingly, the convictions which brought me into republicanism had formed an integral part of my everyday consciousness, my world view. Inevitably, the creative impulse was refracted through these convictions.

However, writing to political prescription risks usurping the humanity which must be primary in any story and which is art's universal appeal. Yet art, which sublimates, illuminates, enriches and celebrates life, also protests against injustice and the wickedness of humankind, and rails with exasperation against a God who presides over senseless suffering.

'Writers are forged in injustice as a sword is forged,' wrote Ernest Hemingway (though he also said, 'There is no left and right in writing. There is only good and bad writing'). And the critic Cyril Connolly also warned that the 'artist should keep himself free from all creed, from all dogma, from all opinion'.

In jail I wrote a second novel, *On the Back of the Swallow*, a gay love story set in an unnamed city (with the geography of Belfast), where there is no communal violence, RUC or IRA, but where society is still intolerant of difference. Two weeks after the book's publication in August 1994 the IRA declared a ceasefire. I was now into the last nine months of my sentence and I dared wonder for the first time if I could give up the commitments I had sworn myself to – now that there was a real chance of peace and the conflict being resolved – and become those magic words, *a writer!*

I doubted if I could. My doubts increased as I watched the peace process flounder. I was in mental turmoil, torn in two directions. I really wanted to write but I couldn't write creatively and be a political activist. It wasn't just a problem of needing time to write, to perfect, to read others and read widely. I required a radical change in my psychology and I knew I was going to disappoint friends and comrades. I had come out of jail middle-aged, divorced, a grandfather and homeless.

In prison I had begun another book, *The Wrong Man*, about an informer: a sympathetic portrayal *à la* Liam O'Flaherty. I was fascinated by the phenomena of temptation and weakness. Acts of minor betrayal, disloyalty, infidelity and hypocrisy, are, after all, common practices in life and might even be considered necessary for getting through life.

I applied to the Arts Council in Dublin for a grant to help me keep my head above water when I was released. They gave me £3,000 – but it was their expression of faith in me that was just as important.

In jail I remember reading a quote in the *Guardian* from a Chinese writer, Zhang Xianliang, who was visiting England. Zhang's father had been arrested and accused of spying, and had died in a Maoist prison in the 1950s. Zhang himself spent twenty-two years in jails and labour camps – his poetry had been judged 'deviant' – until he was rehabilitated. Zhang said: 'Every thinking person has a choice of three different relationships with the society and politics of his or her country: to participate, to flee, or to transcend.'

It was a statement that spoke volumes for the dilemma I was experiencing. I had devoted my entire adult life to the republican movement, had been involved in its politics and development, yet deep down I had always wanted to be a writer, a sort of spokesperson for humankind, a vocation some would say is at odds with the precepts of the armed struggle I defended. It is a criticism I reject and which says more, I believe, about the political prejudices of the commentator.

I had been in the thick of things, in the republican leadership, and had coined the phrase 'the Armalite and the ballot box' to sum up IRA strategy when the debate about Sinn Féin taking part in electoral politics was being held many years ago. The decision to open up an 'electoral front' (though we were not aware of it at the time) and the success of the strategy produced a dynamic that favoured the supremacy of politics. And the transition to politics exclusively, via a peace process and political negotiations, became possible when the British also conceded that there was no military solution, the IRA would not be defeated and they should recognise the legitimacy of the Sinn Féin mandate.

The ceasefires which began in 1994 and my growing sense of independence had allowed me to write much more freely. I felt an ability to be more objective. I wasn't out to defend a cause. I didn't feel the need to write apologias. I was halfway through my third book and eight months out of prison when the IRA ended its ceasefire with the explosion at Canary Wharf in London. I was shattered. I felt that we were in for another twenty-five years of conflict but believed that dialogue was the way forward, the only way forward. I discussed my dilemma with my partner and with my sons. I spoke to writer friends, Dermot Healy, Tim O'Grady and Ronan Bennett. I spoke to my editor and publicist at Mercier Press. And I spoke to Gerry Adams, a friend and confidant, about my divided self. All were sympathetic and very supportive.

So I took the plunge.

You are only on earth once. I was going to become a writer!

I did publicity work for Féile an Phobail (the West Belfast Festival) and started reviewing fiction for magazines and newspapers to help support me as I finished *The Wrong Man* in late 1996. This book dealt with themes of betrayal, infidelity, guilt and the potential that violence has for corrupting the individual. It was published in 1997 and I was pleased with many of the reviews. The *Sunday Times* – no friend of mine – wrote: 'a fast-paced and gut-wrenching examination of the tensions between republican militarism and family life . . . a powerful and complex piece of story-telling.' The *Belfast Telegraph* said: '*The Wrong Man* should come to be regarded as one of the most important books of the Troubles.'

There is a dependent relationship between a writer and his or her society, be that society at war or divided against itself or even at peace. No artist functions in a psychological vacuum and there are pressures to represent the interests of one's community. Some writers simply 'flee', believing that they can transcend history, loyalty and communal solidarity, often to enjoy only illusory objectivity.

We cannot wholly escape our roots, conditioning and upbringing. Edward Said, in *Culture and Imperialism*, quotes Hugo of St Victor, a twelfth-century monk from Saxony, who wrote: 'The person who finds his homeland sweet is still a tender beginner; he to whom every soil is as his native one is already strong; but he is perfect to whom the entire world is as a foreign place.' That sets a huge, almost impossible challenge, given that we are precisely who we are because of parents and siblings, hearth and home, town and country, history, and that it is the streams of sweet and bitter memory that we unceasingly pan for our security and the meaning of our lives.

There is nowhere else to look.

One Wednesday I was in my local shopping centre, where, after I have finished writing for the day, I enjoy spending many of my afternoons in a mood of serendipity, bumping into friends, occasionally seeing former neighbours from Corby Way or school pals, as I do the grocery shopping and think of dinner.

And there she was.

Back on that August night in 1969, when we were standing at the corner, I had seen her before she saw me. I hadn't seen Angela in perhaps twenty-five years. She instantly recognised me and I went over and ostentatiously kissed her on the cheek and asked how things were. For a score of reasons it is obvious that we could never have made a lasting, happy couple. It was just a magnificent instant we shared and, besides, back then and for long afterwards, I was restlessness incarnate.

I broached the subject of that August night and how stupid I had been to spoil it. 'At least I apologised,' I said.

'What do you mean?' she asked.

'I told Rosemary to tell you I was sorry for trying to grope you.'

Her radiant smile lit up the entire world and she started laughing. 'Are you serious? I thought you meant you were sorry because you didn't want to see me again!'

I too laughed, and realised that although that little misunderstanding had cost me dearly, I had secretly relished those bittersweet years, had regretted none of the heartache and the experience that had helped make me the person, the writer, I am.

DOWN TO GROVETREE

It was in the back of a taxi that I last remember having a proper conversation with my mother. She had been complaining of headaches of late and her doctor said her blood pressure was high. It was around October 1981, when the H-Block hunger strike had ended or was ending, and we were coming from the funeral of an old friend of my father's, Jimmy McGivern, whose son was once engaged to my sister Geraldine, and in whose butcher's shop I had worked when I was fifteen and in love with Marian.

I was married and living not far from my parents so we all got out of the taxi together and said our goodbyes. A few days later, I was being interviewed by a television crew outside the Sinn Féin offices on the Falls Road when a car pulled up and a friend, Sheila McVeigh, quickly got out. She told me that my mother had just been rushed to the hospital with a suspected heart attack. The British army had been raiding the republican houses in the street and were heading into ours when my mother collapsed at the front door. I cut short the interview and Sheila and I went to the Royal Victoria Hospital, only to find out that it wasn't their 'take-in' day and that my mother had been admitted to the City Hospital. We went to the City and into the casualty department. I saw my mother lying on a bed, waiting to be attended. I spoke to her but she was completely disorientated and her face was crimson. She was then taken into the theatre.

I was quite nervous about being there and feared assassination because the City Hospital was close to the loyalist Sandy Row, and that year I had been prominent on television during the hunger strike and the by-elections in Fermanagh and South Tyrone. My father came immediately from work and I left to go home and mind my younger brother.

As it turned out my mother had suffered a brain haemorrhage. She was transferred to the Royal Victoria Hospital on the Falls Road, which specialises in neurosurgery, and went through a critical operation. She never recovered and lost her ability to form memories. It was a massive blow to our family but at least she was still alive. She had to be cared for full-time while my father continued to work nights in Telephone House, where he was a deputy supervisor. Although various friends, neighbours and relatives helped out, a lot of the responsibility after his school hours unfairly fell on my young brother Ciaran, who was just thirteen, which represented a reversal of the conventional mother–child relationship.

My mother had no will, had to be told to do things and didn't initiate any conversation. She liked to sleep a lot, and in fact if you turned your head she would be asleep in an instant. The fact that she would never recover sank in slowly. On one occasion, when my sister Margaret was visiting from England, my mother, a heavy woman, slipped and fell in the bathroom and Margaret couldn't lift her. She phoned me. I came immediately to the house and helped her up. But we discovered that she had hurt her ankle and took her to the hospital, where she was admitted for a fracture. Miraculously, as a result of the accident, she came alive and was animated that night. When I visited her she gabbled away about the nursing staff, invented incredible adventures and love affairs between them and whispered that the man opposite, visiting his wife, was in the Special Branch.

I was overjoyed. Even though she was talking gibberish, she was talking. It was as if some wire in her brain that had been severed during her original fall had been reconnected as a result of her accident, and that gave us hope. I phoned my younger sister, Susan, and told her to get down to the hospital as soon as possible to see the change. But by the time she arrived, my mammy had reverted to her silent state. The medical staff explained that the anaesthetic, probably through some side effect, had triggered my mother's activity.

Over the years she put on weight, became ponderous and fell a lot. She couldn't properly negotiate the stairs, required a lot of laundry, and sometimes, half-dressed, she escaped in the early hours and would make her way to her old house in Andersonstown, looking for her mother, who had died in 1959. My father resisted putting her into a residential home for as long as possible, but it was the best decision in the circumstances. There she would receive professional care, though that never stopped us feeling guilty.

She is visited regularly. When you go into the TV lounge, she is usually sitting with her chin tucked into her chest, sleeping soundly. She doesn't know that her youngest daughter, Susan, who had been in need of a heart, lung and liver transplant, died in the autumn of 2001, that my two older sisters and I have all been divorced and two of us have remarried, that Ciaran's been to jail, I've been to jail, my Daddy's moved house, that her sisters May, Anna and Eileen have died, that her brothers Harry and Willie are dead, or that she has great-grandchildren. Nor that her friend in the residential home, Noreen Johnston, has been dead three years. If you ask her where Noreen is, she will say, 'She's around somewhere.' She doesn't know what day it is, does no harm, hurts not a fly, and is in a state of grace, so that when you visit her you feel not just the old affections, but that you are in the presence of innocence incarnate.

You can get her to tell a white lie to reveal how protective she still is of others. If you ask her if anyone was down seeing her last night, she will say no, because she cannot remember. But if you appear annoyed and rejoin with an invention, such as, 'Well, I'd love to know why Eileen McKee told me she was down', she will say, 'Oh yes, what am I talking about, Eileen was here.'

I once did a very stupid thing, thinking that she would understand I was only fooling. I said to her, 'What do you think of my da! He was out gallivanting last night again and left the dance with a big blonde on the end of his arm.' The blood drained from her face and she started to cry like a jilted young girl as I reassured her I was only joking.

I don't believe she did any wrong in her life or broke any hearts. I asked her recently who was the first boy she ever went out with. She thought for a moment: 'Willie McDermott.' Where from? 'Distillery Street,' she replied in an instant. I asked her what age she had been and she said sixteen. My mother at sixteen: a whole universe before her.

Whatever happened to Willie McDermott?

'I don't know,' she said and sank back into silence.

Everywhere she went, she was the life and soul of the party, says my Aunty Kathleen, her sister and four years her junior. Kathleen remembers her in the Club Astor in downtown Belfast getting up for a dare and – sober! – doing a Russian dance on top of a table. They went to the Plaza Ballroom, where they got in free because the bandleader was their brother, Jack White. They thought themselves 'big girls' because they smoked, though I never saw my mother smoke properly. She seemed to kiss and suck rather than deeply inhale the cigarette, then she would blow out the smoke as if she was blowing out a candle.

Her best friend was 'Girlie' Brown. During the war, Girlie's brother was in jail for IRA activities, yet Girlie joined the Auxiliary Territorial Service (part of the Territorial Army). All the girls used to go roller-skating on the Shankill Road, even though Girlie couldn't skate. Kathleen introduced Girlie to an American soldier, GI Frank Falsetto, who couldn't skate either, so the couple sat all night talking. When Girlie married Frank and went off to the USA, I am sure it left a gap in my mother's life. But she was soon married herself and within eight years had four children. When we were kids she talked about Girlie constantly, and they wrote to each other for three decades, until Mammy's brain haemorrhage. Girlie died in September 2002.

I used to dash home from primary school and the first thing I did was put on the radiogramme and change the station from the Home Service to the Light Programme. On one particular day, a Bridie Gallagher song, 'A Mother's Love's a Blessing', was on the radio. My mammy came in from the kitchen and stood, then began sobbing at the chorus, 'You'll never miss your mother's love, Till she's buried beneath the clay.' I asked her what was wrong and she said she missed my granny. I caught her secretly crying quite often for about a year after my Granny White's death.

When I recall the parties in our house in Corby Way, I remember most her singing 'Eileen O'Grady', part of which goes:

> Come, come, beautiful Eileen,
> Out for a drive with me.
> Over the mountain and down by the fountain
> Over the high road and down by the low road.
> Make up your mind,
> Don't be unkind, and we'll drive to Castlebar.
> To the road I'm no stranger
> For you there's no danger,
> So hop like a bird
> On the old jaunty car.

In her seventy-seventh year, after suffering for some time from pyorrhoea, and with many of her teeth reduced to black stumps, she had all her teeth removed. I was visiting her and we were alone in the lounge of the home. I asked her did she remember the words of 'Eileen O'Grady' and her eyes lit up. I coaxed her to sing me a verse and she sang but the words came out gummy and I suddenly realised how old my mother was and I was very sad, because of the course her life had suddenly taken twenty years ago, because I remember her singing and laughing and I remember the young woman who brought me to school on my first day and how I looked back and loved her.

Along with my father, she comes to us on Christmas Day for dinner and will eat the goose and stuffing and sprouts and the Christmas pudding but will not gossip nor ask for any more gravy or ice cream. She has no volition and you are not even sure if putting a party hat on her head and asking her to pull a cracker is fair to her dignity, even though, as I said, she herself was once the life and soul of the party – a singer, a dancer, a joker who now remembers little of twenty minutes ago, never mind twenty years ago.

My mammy never wanted us to leave home, to leave the nest. My late sister Susan was exactly the same a few years ago when her daughter, Cathy, left home for college in Dublin, and later moved to a flat in Belfast. The last time our family was all together for Christmas dinner, before my sisters Margaret and Geraldine went off to England to get married, was thirty years ago. I was seventeen and Ciaran, the baby, was just two.

Although my father worked six days a week and brought in the money, it was Mammy who turned that money into the loving cornucopia that was our simple home – the biscuits in the cupboard, the lemonade in the fridge, the clean clothes that appeared in the wardrobe from nowhere, the made beds.

Santa Claus was now coming for Ciaran alone, but the rest of us also got what we wanted and had been hinting at for weeks in advance. If I close my eyes I can still see her in her apron out in the steaming kitchen, testing the turkey, turning over the roasties, checking the stuffing, baking her own pudding, lifting the lid off a pot, tasting the soup, singing a little song which I think she invented, sometimes biting a nail, uncomplaining, triumphant, and content to be giving herself to us, as if she couldn't give us enough, while we sprawled on the chairs and sofa and fought over the television and gave each other orders.

We all sit at the table like royalty while she serves us and we forget to tell her how good her dinner is and discover only later, and too late, that no one has ever made soup like hers, and that from out of her tiny kitchen she produced a banquet.

In 1916 loyalists drove my Granda and Granny White and their five children out of Blackwater Street. They moved into a Catholic street close by, Ward Street, where my mother was born Susan White in 1924. When she was six they moved to Distillery Street but they were put out of there in the mid-thirties, again by loyalists, and moved to Andersonstown Park, which was then on the city limits. (When Harry was on the run he used the name 'Anderson' for a while and I wonder if that was a little private salute in the direction of home.) Those first two streets she grew up in were knocked down and redeveloped in the 1970s. From the bench in the grounds of her residential home she looks out onto Distillery Street, but doesn't know that this is where she grew up.

Distillery Street, Blackwater Street and Ward Street were offshoots of one of the main arteries through West Belfast, the Grosvenor Road. Her residential home is at the junction of the Grosvenor Road and Cullingtree Road and takes its amalgamated name after them, *Grovetree* House. And that is why, when we are going to visit her, to sit beside her and hold her hand, to talk to her and try to draw out her memories and revisit the past, we just say we're going 'down to Grovetree'.

BIG DAN

The phone rang that Friday morning, around ten. 'Hello, Danny. It's Geraldine.'

'Geraldine? Geraldine who?'

'Geraldine, the home help. I've some bad news for you, Danny. Your daddy's fell down the stairs. Danny, he's dead . . . '

I broke down immediately and began wailing, 'Ah Jesus, no! Ah Jesus, no!' I managed to compose myself for a moment and told Geraldine I'd be there in five minutes. I then phoned my wife and she had to calm me down to understand what I was saying, then I phoned my brother Ciaran who was on a tea-break at work and he too broke down.

My taxi depot sent a car quickly. When I arrived at my daddy's I saw police jeeps parked on either side of the road. Geraldine and a local priest, Father Murphy, were standing in the street and I said something to them, though I can't remember exactly what. The police were in the house and a sergeant opened the door to me. He asked me to be careful and said the sight might upset me. My daddy was lying on his back with his bare feet on the first step of the stairs, his hands open, palms up. In the fall he had cracked the back of his skull on the hall floor – he was a heavy man – and had lost a lot of blood. His face was filled with a defensive grimace, one of preparing for sudden pain, though I imagine he would have been concussed, or would have died almost immediately.

Because of the circumstances of his death, the CID were called in. They photographed the scene and took statements. I covered his body with a sheet and later helped two ambulance men from the morgue lift his body onto a stretcher. It was then that we discovered – underneath his body, on his right side – his shoes and socks, neatly, almost side by side, indicating that he had fallen only a short distance, as otherwise his footwear would have been scattered over several stairs. It appears that he had been carrying them in his right hand and had been holding on to only one banister rail with his left hand when he lost his balance.

He had come home from a pensioners' Christmas party where he had had dinner and drinks. He had sung two love songs: 'Some Enchanted Evening' from *South Pacific* and Ray Charles' 'You Don't Know Me'. Despite being weak on his legs (he had had both his kneecaps replaced) he had also danced. I always loved watching him dance – ballroom or modern, even jiving – as he was always self-assured. Over the years I tried to dance like him but he was inimitable. Even when overweight, he had a way of moving gracefully – of rolling just his top half from side to side a little – so that his poor partner did most of the work, but the spotlight magically remained on him. Sometimes he made faces to the ceiling or to the wings behind his partner's back, or pinched his nose with his finger and thumb while flushing a chain with his free hand in an impish gesture that indicated she had a few dance classes yet before her. The audience loved it.

His friends said he had enjoyed himself at that Christmas party. But for the previous two months, since the death of my sister Susan, he had been very down.

Visiting me in jail in 1991, Susan, who was then thirty-four, told me that the doctors had diagnosed her with a progressive liver disease, primary biliary cirrhosis (PBC), which would kill her within five years if she didn't have a transplant. PBC has no known cause or cure. Susan had been aware of this for over a year but she and her husband John had kept it a secret. She was now telling the family only because it was visibly affecting her stamina and lifestyle.

She soldiered on, had her condition regularly monitored and tried experimental drugs, many of which made her lethargic and sick. She managed to slow down the progress of the disease, but then was struck with rheumatoid arthritis. She developed an itch all over her body and wanted to rip the flesh from herself. A year before she died, her condition deteriorated rapidly, and in hospital, during tests, she suffered a mild stroke. She was rushed to Papworth Hospital in Cambridgeshire, where specialists told her that it was not just a liver transplant she now needed, but a triple transplant including lungs and heart. The waiting list was long, there would be problems getting matching organs and there was a high rate of rejection. Susan's morale plummeted. She suffered greatly for the last twelve months of her life, regularly having to be woken during the night to inhale drugs through a nebuliser, and John, who cared for her devotedly, had to give her daily injections in her stomach.

John and Susan married when she was only sixteen and John was twenty-one. About eighteen months before her death, I remember us all out together, in a club. Though exhausted, she asked John up to dance to Shania Twain's song, 'You're Still the One'. The pair made good dancers and I saw Susan look into John's eyes as she mimed the lyrics:

> They said, 'I bet they'll never make it.'
> But just look at us holding on,
> We're still together, still going strong.

Racked with pain, and in between stays in hospital, Susan somehow kept a little bit of stamina in reserve to see her son Gary and Joanne get married, though by then she was on oxygen and in a wheelchair. On 28 October 2001, two weeks after the wedding, with John by her hospital bedside, she died. It was a Sunday morning. He telephoned me with the news and I went to my daddy's. I had to wait until he returned from Mass. I heard him outside saying good morning to a neighbour. He put the key in the door, came through the hall, hung up his walking stick, then expressed surprise at seeing me at this unusual time. I kept up a façade until he was in the living room and close to a chair.

And then I told him.

It's painful even now to recall the look on his face, his initial gasp of, 'Good God, no,' and the long silence which followed as he sank into his chair, unable to speak.

Our Susan was attractive, without spite, forgiving, kind and loving. Having said that, she was no walkover. She decided what to do with her life, had no regrets that I know of and was a trustworthy confidante. She would tell you a few home truths about yourself and point out any hypocrisy or double standards. She was the angel of our family. Because of circumstances – my sisters Geraldine and Margaret living in England, Ciaran in England for a while before returning home, myself absorbed with republicanism (and married with two boys), Ciaran and I, both later imprisoned – it was Susan who carried not only her own home but also my daddy's after Mammy's brain haemorrhage. Until her condition handicapped her physically, she used to travel twice a week – a total of fifty-six miles, often by public transport – to my da's to clean the house, wash and iron the clothes and do his serious shopping.

No wonder they were so close.

When we drove up to Susan's wake my daddy said, 'You aren't supposed to bury your children; they're supposed to bury you.' Then tears ran down his cheek and Ciaran and I quietly cried.

We waked my da in the house he had bought in December 1986. He had moved because our former home in the next street, Iveagh Parade, still had an outside toilet. Renovation work, including living in a mobile home for several months, would have been too disruptive for Mammy, so it was easier to sell up and shift. It was such a short move that my mates and I, including Kevin Brady, who was to be killed by Michael Stone a year later in Milltown Cemetery, were able to carry practically all the furniture to the new house. The furniture included big wardrobes the rector of Clonard Monastery had given my daddy and Uncle Seamus in the early sixties in partial lieu of payment for painting work they carried out.

When I was separated I used to spend the weekends in the new house in Iveagh Drive with my two sons, but apart from those times with them, the house held no memories of places where we kids all grew up together before leaving for the world, unlike the others in Iveagh Parade and Corby Way.

I was fairly dazed during the wake and later found it difficult to piece together who had been condoling with us at what time or on what day. We were comforted by the large procession of people who passed through the house, including old neighbours from Andersonstown, which we had left almost forty years before.

Friends of my da's from his days in the shipyard and Telephone House paid their respects.

Because he was being buried on Christmas Eve there was a problem with flights, and Daddy's two sisters, Eileen in New Zealand and Margaret in the USA, were unable to attend. My sister Geraldine, husband John and daughter Sharon weren't able to make it to the house before the final prayers and the coffin lid was screwed down and we looked upon him for the last time – on this earth, at least.

My wife whispered to me that we should toast him goodbye with a bottle of his Powers whiskey, just as Joe Slovo's relatives had said their farewell to him in celebration of his life. But I told her that we couldn't do that because Ciaran and Margaret, amongst others present, would be taking Holy Communion.

I had argued that we shouldn't tell Mammy. It would probably only distress her – if even for only ten or fifteen minutes, until she forgot – but might do worse damage. The family agreed, some with misgivings. We asked the staff of Grovetree House to ask other residents not to mention it to her.

So Mammy wasn't at the funeral.

It took six of us at a time to carry him: the first lift was taken by Susan's John and our cousin Seamus White at the front; Daddy's two brothers, Jimmy and Gerard, in the middle; and Ciaran and I at the back. Requiem Mass was held in St Paul's, where he was baptised. He was buried in my Granda Morrison's grave in Milltown Cemetery.

Afterwards, we went to one of my daddy's haunts, the

West Social Club, for refreshments. I asked Jimmy and Gerard did they get the photocopies of the article about my Granda Morrison's younger brother William, who had been killed by the British army in 1922, which I gave to my da for them. It turned out he hadn't sent them. I knew at the time he was annoyed. He had insisted that his grandfather was a tailor who could have easily afforded to bury his son and there was no way William would have been buried or would have been allowed to be buried in a pauper's grave. It remains a mystery.

Jimmy and Gerard had more information on their father. They said he was a Celtic football fanatic. (My da had no interest in sport, apart from greyhound and horse racing.) When my granda was demobbed at the end of the First World War at a camp in Finaghy, Belfast, he worked for the US government, tailoring and shortening the tunics of US officers to make them more like those worn by British soldiers.

I told Jimmy about my granda being arrested in 1922 and he said that somewhere along the line he had heard he was in the IRA and had trained behind Black Mountain. He confirmed that he had also joined the Free State army but had deserted. In the army he had boxed and he had one fight in Monaghan, on which a lot of money was wagered. He was being slaughtered during the first two rounds and was told to take a dive but refused. In the third round he caught his opponent with a sucker punch and knocked him out. He and a friend had to clear out of town because the fight was supposed to have been fixed. They ditched their uniforms in the railway station and returned to Belfast in civvies. Granda also loved snooker and was nicknamed 'Blackball' because once he got on the table he pocketed all the balls in succession until he finished on the black.

When the Second World War broke out he rejoined the RAF; he was based in Malta from 1939 to 1942, before being discharged on medical grounds in 1944. He was a compulsive smoker and would 'suck a Woodbine until it was a stump', according to Jimmy. No wonder he died young, at sixty-two. His wife, Ellen, lived for another thirty-seven years.

I have few memories of my father from 17 Corby Way, the two-bedroom house where I was born and spent the first three or four years of my life. I can look at old photographs, about which family members have told stories from time to time, even photographs in which I feature, but I can't be certain that I wouldn't merely be repeating their memories.

I remember toing and froing on a door swing on a sunny day when Geraldine, aged six, and Margaret, aged four, declared that they had had enough of my mammy and were going to go live with Granny Morrison or Granny White. 'Go right ahead,' said my mother, who even packed them a small suitcase. I was terrified that something was getting out of hand yet thrilled that I would have Mammy to myself (unaware that she was carrying Susan). They left and turned the corner, sat down on a small wall and cried before returning and declaring that they were sorry and wanted to stay. That's my memory of it, though my sisters would have perhaps a more graphic, accurate picture of the occasion. It might even have happened during one of those times when Daddy was away in England working.

We moved from No. 17 to No. 2 with the help of a fleet of neighbours who carried the furniture down the street. I now had my own room.

I used to think we got our first television when my daddy won a bet on the Grand National and came home like a hero, carrying the TV on top of his shoulder. I asked him about this not long before he died. It was not on a horse race, but at Dunmore Park greyhound track that he had accumulated his winnings and it was on the Shankill Road that he bargained down the price of a television for cash. It was delivered to our house by my granda in his van. We were one of the first houses in Corby Way to have a television. The Ulster Television station had just begun broadcasting, and when my da came in from work he had to negotiate his way through the bodies of all our friends lying on the floor watching *Ivanhoe* or *Robin Hood*.

My da was tall, though in old age he shrank. He cycled to work in the shipyard, came home at night for his dinner, then cycled back if there was overtime. He also worked on Saturday mornings, and in recent years used to tease me over my writing, saying that I didn't know what real work was. One Friday night he hid his bike in an entry close to Celtic Park, went in to watch 'the dogs', gambled and lost most of his money. When he came through the door, my mammy read his sheepish look instantly. When he told her that he had lost his money *and* his bike, she got stuck into him and shouted that they hadn't even got his bus money to work. When things like that happen, and you're a kid, you think you are about to become a refugee.

On another day Mammy told me to go and meet him in Bearnagh Drive as he came home from work. I spotted him in the distance from his long overcoat and cap and confident stride and ran up to him. He always smelt of linseed oil from the putty he used at work; even his lunchbox smelt of linseed. It was my birthday. From beneath his coat he took out a puppy and asked me what I wanted to call it. He had painted the *Canberra* and other boats called the Prince of this or the Prince of that, and I shouted, 'Call him Prince!' On my previous birthday or for Christmas – I can't be sure which – he spent his nights in the coalhouse, over a period of a week or two, making me a huge wooden fort (I was into cowboys and Indians), painstakingly cutting out the crenels and making a stockade, then varnishing it.

When Prince came along I turned the fort into an open kennel and put down a blanket. I had been quite proud of my daddy for making me that fort and just a few years ago, attempting to deepen our limited rapport, I was reminiscing about it when he said he hadn't a clue what I was talking about. He could remember no fort. Could he have completely forgotten? Surely my perfect description of its appearance, my enthusiasm in recalling his sawing and gluing, him down on his knees on those cold nights, should have fired some embedded memory?

I know there are things we easily forget, do forget, choose to forget, especially if they pain or embarrass or shame us, but not fond memories. Forgetting is a defence mechanism; it allows us to get away with stealing, adultery – killing, even. It is the antithesis of conscience. And if we can forget our grievous wrongs, how much more easy it is to forget about the throwaway or careless remark which leaves the invisible wound. In my teens I had a close friend, Bobby, whom I mentioned in the prologue. As I became more involved in republicanism, we drifted apart. I hadn't spoken to him in about twenty years until we met at the funeral of a mutual acquaintance, Jimmy Green. I had never known Bobby to take alcohol but after the funeral we went to a club for a drink. He is two years older than me. We used to go to Mass together, went for walks and went to dances. Because he was shy, he never got up to dance and he rarely left anyone home. He probably viewed me as promiscuous – though this was far from the truth.

He said that one day we were walking through the Falls Park debating life and love and that I crushed him by saying – and contrasting me to him – that 'an ounce of experience is worth a ton of advice'. Now, I remember that phrase and I remember having used it at one time or many times. But as soon as he said what he said I knew he was telling the truth. I had used it against him, I had been nasty and egotistic. I had wanted to put him down because he had been moralising at me. What could he tell me about life and love, I had thought contemptuously. In one quickly forgotten remark, I had been cruel, and he had carried this bitter memory around from 1971 until 1997, when I finally apologised, he accepted, and the hurt was laid to rest.

Every summer my Da had two weeks off work – over the 'Twelfth fortnight'. We went to Uncle Harry's in Dublin a few summers in succession. Another time, we rented a cottage in Glenarm village for a week. One year, when money was scarce, we went on day trips, and on one of these occasions he took us up to Parliament Buildings at Stormont for a conducted tour. I got to sit in the Speaker's Chair. Stormont was detested by nationalists, so it was a strange place to bring us. But he also brought us to watch the Orangemen march through Belfast on 12 July, and waved at people he knew, and to the Lord Mayor's parade, which was also considered to be an exclusively unionist event.

At home, it was my mammy who did the chastising, who would lose her temper and smack you with her hand, or whatever was nearest to hand. Then she'd immediately be sorry. My Da never once struck me. When the Troubles broke out we argued over politics. He wrongly blamed old Jimmy Green for getting me involved in republicanism. He was totally opposed to violence, couldn't understand my preoccupation with politics, and emphasised that wife, children and home came before everything else.

We argued most often when he came home from the Pigeon Club, his local, which he visited around half ten every night after working in Telephone House. The late news would come on and this would be my opportunity to whisper under my breath or say something provocative about the Brits – how indefensible their actions were. Mammy would be making faces to get me to shut up. Sometimes he would be accompanied by a work colleague, Tony Teague, and I'd get them both going. Tony would go home swearing that I was trouble and I was mad, then my Da would insist that we get down and say the Rosary, and to appease him I would. Geraldine and Margaret had, by this time, left for England. Susan was fourteen, and Ciaran three. I was eighteen, at college, doing A-levels, but had started skipping days and was about to start working full-time in the movement. For months afterwards, when I was active, my daddy still thought I was at college.

About a year later he was visiting me in Long Kesh, where I was interned, and he said: 'Is it still freezing in there? Is there still a huge draught between the two doors?' I was taken aback and said, 'Why? Were you interned here as well?' He laughed. 'When I joined the RAF I did my induction up here.' Now, I must have been told about him having been in the RAF (he worked as an 'aircraft finisher', painting the planes) – it's not the type of thing that could be kept a secret – but I was astonished and it came to me as news. He joked that he had joined in June 1944 when he was certain that the war was over: he wanted to be a 'Brylcreem Kid' – presumably a nickname for service people. There is a photograph of him in my Mammy's room in Grovetree wearing his RAF beret, and he looks quite handsome. He was discharged in May 1946.

When they were young he took my two older sisters to see *South Pacific* and other Rodgers and Hammerstein musicals. Going through the house and dividing up mementoes and photographs, we came across the sheet music to *South Pacific*, which Geraldine has now kept.

We also came across love letters he had written to my mammy in the 1950s from England. There was no painting work in Belfast and he had to go to Bury and work as a labourer in the Manchester area. He stayed with his sister Eileen, her husband Albert and their children Carol and Stephen. 'Glad to hear that you are sending me some things. As you probably know, I left home with just the one pair of trunks, no towel or handkerchiefs, one pair of socks. I have been wearing Albert's every time I have a change.' He talks about how cold winter is and that he would love her to come over and visit him. (They save up and she eventually does.) He buys a pair of shoes for two pounds, nine shillings and sixpence, 'and they have left me practically broke, so I will have to start and save up the boat fare at Easter, which I am looking forward to with all my heart.'

He had wanted Mammy to go and live in England but she would not leave Belfast, probably because of her family but also because I think she was attached to *homeland* in a way that the Morrisons were not. Had she agreed, what views would I have ended up with, in addition to my English accent?

He gets up at 5 AM and catches a bus to Radcliff. He works at loading bales of wood pulp from lorries all day long. 'As regards my work, I don't like it at all. You have to work too hard for the few halfpence they pay you, but there is nothing I can do about it. I will just have to stick it out until things brighten up in the shipyard.'

My Uncle Harry cracked a joke to my mammy about having driven my da to leave. She told him what Harry said and he responds angrily:

> . . . it's because I like to see my family eating and living half decently that I was forced to come over here and earn a few shillings to keep them, for I could never reconcile myself to go on the dole, and to go about touching my relations for food for you and the kids . . .
>
> PS I am enclosing £4 in this letter. Do your best with it as it is all I could sub of my wages.

He tells Mammy how much he loves coming in at night around seven and seeing a letter from her on the sideboard. But he also complains when she doesn't write daily, or enough, or isn't in his mother's when he has arranged to phone! It reminded me of the insecurity of prisoners, who never feel that letters to their loved ones have been properly answered.

> You have said the snag is that there isn't any news to tell me in your letters. Well, can't you just tell me how you get each day in, what you've done, where you've been, what you're going to do, etc., about your family, about the kids, about my family, about the neighbours, so on and so on. And when

you have run out of chat, how much you miss me, how you long to see me, how much you love me, how happy you'll be when I'm home again, and even then you can tell me about the weather.

Most nights he goes to bed early, and it's there that he writes his letters.

Glad to hear that I am constantly in your thoughts, for you are always in mine. I try to picture what you are doing. For instance, right now it is 8.45 PM, I'm in bed writing to you. I'm wondering if you are perhaps this minute writing to me, or thinking of me.

About work he says:

It's hard to go into a strange job with especially strange people. They all resent you until you get into their way of going. I suppose they are afraid that we will work them out of their jobs. You have to have a neck like a rhinoceros for they laugh and wink amongst themselves every time you make a mistake, try to make little of you. But when you let them know you're not a fool, stand up for yourself and even let them have a piece of your mind, or even better still a punch on the nose, they know to respect you and they soon give over playing the monkey. Of course, it's the same in Belfast, you'll get it no matter where you go.

He is, as ever, conscientious about church.

I have just come in from chapel tonight. We had Mass here at 8 PM for the workers, so you see we are better off here than at home, for I never heard yet of an evening Mass at home. And better than that you have to be only fasting from 6 o'clock to receive Holy Communion. But there is a snag. That is, there are four collections at every Mass. Cost you fourpence to get in, two collections inside the church, and one when you are leaving the church . . . in fact, going to church tonight has left me without a penny. I'll have to borrow my bus money for work in the morning from Albert.

He was earning eight pounds a week, sending five to Mammy, paying two pounds to Eileen and then had one pound left for cigarettes and bus fares.

He asks after his kids:

I suppose Margaret's still as loveable as ever. I shouldn't be at all surprised if Danny has forgotten all about me. Tell them all I was asking about them, and that I pray for them and you every night before I go to bed.

Sorry to hear that Geraldine is bad again. Hope it is not necessary for her to go into hospital again. Tell her her daddy was asking about her and hopes that she will be better soon and to write him another letter.

Tell me how you and the kids got Christmas over. Did they like their dolls?

He went out a few times to a local pub and to the cinema. On one occasion Mammy tells him that she went out to a dance and he is clearly hurt.

My da loved the horses and in one letter, in March 1955, he writes:

The Grand National is on at Aintree on Saturday. It costs you five shillings and ninepence return by coach to get there. I would love to go and see it, but I can't afford to have Saturday off, because I have to save up the boat fare. But anyway I shall be backing Quare Times, for surely these are the quarest times we have had since we have been married. I don't suppose you thought that I would ever have to come here for work, for when I was warning you about a probable pay-off you used to say, You haven't been paid off yet so what are you worrying about. Remember?

Quare Times won.

But the letter in which he expresses most joy is after he learns that there is work once again for him in Belfast:

> Well, that was certainly the best news I have heard for a long time on the phone last night and I shall be glad to get back home to you again. I gave my week's notice in this morning and this week will not go in quick enough for me . . . I feel a lot happier and more jubilant now that I know that I'll be able to stop at home and to be with you and the children again. I felt in great form all day and I don't think anything could put me in bad form this week for it must end soon and then the boat home to you again. I just can't wait. So, I shall say goodnight and God bless you and the children and roll on Friday.

Only one letter from my Mammy to Daddy seems to have survived and that's the last one. In it she writes:

> The kids are all delighted that you are coming home for good and I needn't tell you that I am too for I am sure you know it.
>
> Margaret sat up in bed last night with her eyes shining and said, 'Mammy now we'll all be happy, that my Daddy's coming.'

When I got married in 1974, and even after I moved into a house with my wife, where I lived under a false name for several years, I always used my mother and father's address for official business. When the British army raided the house and asked for Danny Morrison and my da appeared, they would arrest him, even though there were differences of twenty-seven years and seven stone between us. It was only when he arrived at the barracks that the intelligence officer would look at him and claim it was a mistake, but it didn't prevent such incidents recurring.

One morning I arrived into the house just after the postman. My daddy had opened a letter from the Royal Victoria Hospital. He was perplexed and shaking his head. I asked him what was the matter and he said that he couldn't understand the letter because it said his sperm count was nil. I quickly took it from him – I had had a vasectomy about a month earlier and was awaiting the all clear. He said to me, half in disbelief, 'You didn't go and do *that*, did you?' I said yes and he said he didn't agree with it.

My daddy had his own close circle of senior citizens, some of whom knew him differently, as a more dynamic person, than his children did. It is not that surprising when you think about it: in our day we kept secrets from our parents and loved ones, and still keep secrets from each other. Maybe our secrets make up our true identity. I remember once telling him that I had just met for the second time (the first occasion was briefly, when he was still an infant) my son, Michael, then in his mid-twenties, who was born to a former girlfriend while I was interned in 1973. He was totally stunned and said he hadn't known he had a grandson that age: my mother had kept it a secret. And he asked me why I had not introduced them – for which I had no answer.

At the wake a few of his friends spoke to him aloud: 'Who's going to sing with us now?' 'Why did you go and leave us?' 'Who am I going to dance with now?' His friend, John Larkin, aged eighty, was in bits. A neighbour, Joe Curran, who daily placed my da's bets for him and brought him the *Irish News*, said to Ciaran and me, 'Do you really know your da? Do you?' suggesting that there was a substantial side to him we didn't know and my da didn't feel free to communicate.

I was to think about that question often in the days and

weeks that followed. I cried many times and couldn't sleep properly for a month. I kept going over his influences on me, and my rejection of some of his values. He tried to keep his emotional cards close to his chest but was a mix of romantic and cynic, and he was, deep down, unable to repress his romantic nature. Between 1950 and 1971 his two sisters and two brothers, and his mother, left Ireland for good. But on Christmas Night or St Stephen's Night, before they left, they would regularly come to our house for drinks. On one occasion we were watching *Holiday Inn* on television, with the lights down. When Bing Crosby sang 'White Christmas' I noticed that my da had a tear in his eye. In one of his love letters to my mammy he writes enthusiastically about having just been to the pictures and seen *Holiday Inn*. I am now wondering if when watching the film again, ten years later, he was emotional because he recalled just how lonely he had been, that time in England, without her. Mammy's illness, her loss of will, of memory, her inability to initiate conversation or exchange affection undoubtedly left a huge gap in his life, a loneliness that we didn't perhaps appreciate. He was only fifty-five when the substance of her was cut off from us.

No doubt there was much about him that went over our heads, either because we took him for granted or gave up on him, because he was taciturn by day and extrovert only by night when he was with his circle and we were not around. Besides, we were preoccupied with our own struggles. People to whom we are too close often appear one-dimensional and we are surprised when we realise how many other lives they touch or the variety of people they interest, just as, when some jaded lover with whom we have broken up appears with someone new, we are suddenly reminded of their qualities. This is the way I felt when his many, many friends called to the house to tell us that he was a gentleman or that 'you'll never be half the man your da was.'

I began to think about our relationship, how close we really were. I also experienced some guilt at not having visited him or socialised with him more often. I had promised to do some of the housework when Susan was no longer able to help but had helped out only occasionally.

When I talked to friends, one told me that his father died five years ago and that there isn't a day goes by that he doesn't think about him. His father had a lingering death and he told me that he helped him to die. Another e-mailed me in response to an obituary I had written in my local newspaper and wrote that I obviously had a high regard and respect for my father. 'I never really liked mine and couldn't build any kind of relationship with him,' he said. 'Yet, after his death, nine or so years later, I often think about him, about times as a youngster with him, about his real effect on my life, about the regret at not under-standing him, not to mention the guilt at never trying to do so. If that's the case with me, then I imagine it must be altogether worse for you. Your article about him was very moving and brought a tear to my eye, despite never having met the man.'

My da would always keep my ego in check. If he said nothing about my weekly article in the *Andersonstown News* I knew he liked it. But there were many times when he would tell me that what I wrote was 'crap'. In addition, he didn't like my second novel about the gay hero: perhaps that's that generation for you.

There were certainly a few songs and dances in him yet and that is the real tragedy. But for a minor decision – to carry his shoes and socks upstairs, instead of leaving them at the side of his chair downstairs – he might be alive today.

On New Year's Eve we decided to go out to a party for some respite, and toasted all our loved ones, but in particular our parents, to whom we owe the world.

'Auld Lang Syne', Old Long Since, Times Past. And Ciaran, my brother, sang a few verses of one of my father's favourite songs, 'Stardust' by Nat King Cole:

> And now the purple dusk of twilight time
> Steals across the meadows of my heart,
> High up in the sky, the little stars climb
> Always reminding me that we're apart.
>
> You wandered down the lane and far away,
> Leaving me a song that will not die.
> Love is now the stardust of yesterday,
> The music of the years gone by.

AFTERLIFE

After Susan's death I began to think over the old question of God's existence. The idea of God and the Catholic religion were well drilled into me as an impressionable child, but over time I came to reject many tenets of that faith. As I grew older and became more questioning, I realised that my guess about the nature of God and life after death was as valid as any theologian's.

At sixteen I had a major spiritual experience. I had been studying books on yoga and self-hypnotism. This incident sounds so bizarre that in the years since, for fear of being ridiculed, I have described it to a mere handful of confidants.

When my father was redecorating and furniture was being moved about, I had to take my mother's Singer sewing machine into my bedroom, which was at the back of the house, overlooking the entry. It sat along the window. It had a black-lacquered, sturdy wooden box-cover. Late one night, 6 July 1969, to be precise, I couldn't sleep. I climbed out of bed, opened my curtains and was convinced that something important was going to happen. I don't know why, but I sat on top of the box-cover and stared at the sky for some time, trying to break free from the normal distractions of consciousness. Suddenly, my surroundings vanished and I was filled with a mystical presence which in my mind's eye took on the image of the Christ with outstretched hands that we have become used to through iconography, and I felt that the presence was pleased with me. I felt a rush of intense happiness. I felt as if I had seen God. I felt as if I was in heaven. It lasted a split second, then vanished and I tumbled back into myself and felt utterly lonely. I wanted to go with it. I fell to the floor and started crying uncontrollably. My father must have awoken. He came into the room, switched on my light and began to calm me down but I wasn't making sense. I was vaguely aware of Margaret, Geraldine or Susan on the landing asking what was wrong and my father shooing them back to bed.

I blubbered that I had seen God. My father said something about me dreaming or having had a nightmare and he asked me to return to bed, which I did. I was now embarrassed and said I was okay. We never mentioned it again.

The experience was very real to me – even if it was all inside my head. Had it been supernatural, should I not have had an unassailable religious conviction, become apostolic, joined an order or become a priest (or even become a markedly good person)? In fact, the following summer for a short time I rejected the whole notion of God, declaring that I was an atheist, only to return to the conviction of the existence of God – but without being able to plot any further than that.

Following the spiritual experience, through contemplation I was able to experience a great surge of euphoria occasionally, although I never attributed those to any divine communication. But I lost that ability after about two years.

I was reading a book in Long Kesh around 1973. It might have been *The Devils of Loudun* by Aldous Huxley. I came across the word 'theophany', which means a visible manifestation of a deity, and thought that that might have been what I had seen. A priest was visiting me. We were walking around the yard and I brought the conversation around to this subject. I said to him that I thought I might have experienced a theophany, expecting him to be startled and to give me inside information. I might as well have said 'I think I have chilblains', because he just continued talking about something else.

One night, many years later, when my parents were on holiday and I had their house to myself, I was in their bed with a woman to whom I was very close, and with a few drinks on me, told her the story of 6 July. There are certain confessions that lovers make in bed and this should not have been one of them. She listened but said nothing and may have marked me down as doolally. When I next saw my brother Ciaran, a day or two later, he said to me, 'Here, that was some yarn you told your woman about you on top of the sewing machine when God appeared. Did it work?'

My first thought was that the woman had betrayed my confidence. I asked him what he meant. He said that he was in bed in the next room with another woman and could hear everything, and they had to bite the pillowcase to stop themselves from laughing.

It can't be surprising that people might laugh at the implausibility of the story, although many who might dismiss such phenomena are the very same people who uphold Biblical truth (prophecies, miracles) despite the fact that the *New Testament* was written perhaps a hundred years after the events it describes (though with 'God's hand' on the pen, our religious instructor at school, with little conviction, assured us). So, if God is *really* interested in saving our souls – according to Christians that's why Jesus Christ came to earth – why does God make it so hard to believe?

In my system of belief I have God creating the world but I don't know why God did so. God left no link, no connection, no explanation; withdrew, left us struggling to find meaning; left evolving humankind (and, I presume, intelligent life in whatever form wherever throughout the universe) guessing, exasperated and vulnerable to theological charlatans of every kind, so that we can never tell who is a true or false prophet, we can only resort to unscientific faith. We are innately driven to find meaning in life and trying to live a meaningful life without ever knowing if, when and where we were right, until after death, if at all.

I can't believe that life arose accidentally, without purpose. Most people – apart from some terminally ill people, suicides and heroes – have a will to live, possibly based on fear of death, the unknown, but also because life has promise, it feels like a gift, it can be wonderful. The universe has a beauty of design whose mysteries enthral us, as summed up by D. H. Lawrence in his last work, *Apocalypse*, written when he was dying:

> For man, the vast marvel is to be alive. For man, as for flower and beast and bird, the supreme triumph is to be most vividly, most perfectly alive. Whatever the unborn and the dead may know, they cannot know the beauty, the marvel of being alive in the flesh. The dead may look after the afterward. But the magnificent here and now of life in the flesh is ours, and ours alone, and ours only for a time. We ought to dance with rapture that we should be alive and in the flesh, and part of the living, incarnate cosmos.

The idea of the existence of God has stubbornly persisted. It could be an invention with roots in a mix of psychological necessity, history or myth, which, of course, does not necessarily invalidate the existence of God. Organised religion has emerged in all humankind's ages and cultures. Its main constituent is faith.

In contradiction to the idea of a good God there is the cold, random cruelty of nature and the deliberate evil associated with humankind, which leads on to the paradox that if God created everything, he also created evil, therefore he cannot be good. Any one of us can carry out evil acts and we can tell God to go and fuck and nothing happens. So, where is God and what is God doing? You can gas six million people, rape and pillage, and nobody stops you and you might even escape justice catching up with you.

Belief in God assumes a respect for God, a love in gratitude for the gift of life, and a fear of God's omnipotence and retribution; that there could be a divine intervention in your life or in life and that prayer has certain power; that God can see into your mind, heart and soul, can cut through the façade you present to the world; that you could be punished now or later for wrong deeds. These assumptions about what God's 'laws' consist of often overlap or contradict the variety of humankind's morals.

Religion, morality and social norms can be weak forces that only partially circumscribe our thoughts, words and deeds. There is pleasure in light but there is piquancy in darkness. Many of us oscillate between two poles. We become our own God, believe in our own sovereignty, in the primacy of ourselves, and think that no other intelligence can penetrate our inner being and that the real struggle is with the external world and humankind. Then we often collapse into doubt, cowardice and abasement, seeking the help of God out of fear of the retribution from, or the opprobrium of, humankind.

I would like to think that my belief in God has made me act wisely or morally, has curbed some of my actions or had me baulk at certain dubious ones. But on many occasions it hasn't. Even before Machiavelli put *The Prince* into words it was obvious that ruling a country, engaging in politics and waging war are inevitably dirty trades, which sit uncomfortably, if not impossibly, beside the concept of morality. In conflict, the only way to defy and override moral doubt in the interests of politics, or to carry out a grievous act, is to squeeze God out of the equation and consciously act with hubris, on the basis of self-assertion. I cannot abide the hypocrisy of those (and I suspect they form an overwhelming majority) who claim the certainty of God on their side when our purchase on knowledge is so tenuous and limited and quite often we cannot even know the implications of what we are doing.

Away from politics and conflict, at a personal level, one is capable of another type of ruthlessness, of sheer abandonment, rebelliously dining on free will and skating over the feelings or interests of others in celebration of the self: this is my decision, my life, and Fate I defy you. But then, in a mental mess, many limp back home to God, beg for help, ask for forgiveness (though it is other people that have been offended or profaned) and promise to try and be better people.

The religious believe that if we obey God's will (though your guess at what that might be is as good as anyone else's) we will be rewarded after death; we will go, for want of a better word, to heaven. If we have sinned and not paid for our sins on this earth we will pay after death, which means that our souls will suffer. My friend Billy and my wife Leslie, both atheists, cannot take me seriously when I talk about an afterlife, though Billy said casually one night, 'I wonder if oul Maureen is looking down at me and seeing the oul fool I am' (he couldn't remember where he left his watch, then he couldn't remember which of his brothers was nicknamed 'the joiner').

I speculate about the state in which the dead might still exist in a non-material, spiritual world.

If there is divine justice, judgement and punishment, what form does the punishment or suffering take? Are any souls (for want of a better word) in a state of eternal damnation? Can Hitler and his predecessors be forgiven?

How can our lives be good if we have done irreparable wrongs for which we are not sorry or about which we qualify our regret?

Are those who are happiest the ones who were humble and full of humility on earth, who harmed or offended the least, who suffered injustice and died in poverty or were deprived because the advantaged or ruthlessly intelligent manipulated society? Are they in a type of collective trance, or are they still individuals, with their old consciousnesses? Are they in such communion with God that they are in a state of omniscience? Can they see into our minds, into the past, and what fuckers we were to them? Can they see the thoughts we hid from them, our bad sides? Can they see into the future and the harmful steps we might take unless diverted, and can they, out of love for us, intervene (but without our knowing)?

And what of those innocents, such as people with Down's Syndrome, who are beyond malice and evil? In the afterlife do their souls continue in their same pure and naive state or do they enter into an intellect that was denied them on earth? And what of stillborn children who had no experiences and no engagements? Do they become possessed of the skills of communication or is it a mistake to view the condition of the afterlife as a continuation of life as we know it?

And what of the clinically insane, dangerous or innocuous, who do not relate to society, are clearly incapable of relating to this world and are largely not responsible for their actions, however horrific? Do they, after death, see the light, and join with the saved, to use that pejorative word?

William James, author of that wonderful book *The Variety of Religious Experience*, and brother of the writer Henry James, promised his wife and brother that he would try to communicate with them from beyond the grave. William had a lifelong interest in extra-sensory perception and extra-human experience. His interest would appear to have been just life-long. When he died they heard nothing from him.

Was he not allowed to come back? Is that part of the mystery of the condition?

Deirdre, who is married to my brother Ciaran, was alone in my daddy's house shortly after his death. She heard footsteps on the stairs and the sound of doors opening upstairs. She became afraid and fled the house. A few weeks later my son was sleeping in the house and he says that he heard footsteps on the stairs and that it frightened him. I said it was probably the noise from the stairs next door but then remembered that their stairs are on the far side. The noise could have been something as simple as the wood contracting when the temperature dropped.

One night in her sleep Deirdre became hysterical and woke Ciaran up. He eventually calmed her. She told him that my daddy had come to her in her dreams and he said that she was correct, she had heard him on the stairs. He said he had lost something but couldn't find it, that he was dead and, he joked, he was going to have to start acting like he was dead! He said that Susan and he were very happy and that Deirdre shouldn't be afraid, he would not be back.

By definition a ghost cannot do anything physical (except perhaps cause us to tremble and our hearts to palpitate). There have been no proofs of divine intervention, though the Catholic Church believes in miracles and makes saints out of those who led exemplary lives and in whose names, after their death, miracles are said to have been performed. All miracles are open to dispute and in the end belief in them is a matter of faith.

Susan requested that a song by Queen be played at her funeral.

'These Are the Days of Our Lives' was written by the terminally ill Freddie Mercury, and was his swansong. It's about how youth and life quickly pass, about wistfully looking back on sunnier times and how we should be content to watch resemblances of our youth played through our children and enjoyed. And for Susan personally, it was about still loving John, with whom she came through the adventure of her life.

I think of Susan as still existing somewhere out there, being in a better place where she no longer suffers, enjoying good company and, like those with whom she shares peace, able to glimpse something of our unsettled lives below, communicating with us and giving us strength, should we care to look, in the many great examples the dead have left us of how to live, how to forgive and how to love.

Afterword

In the opinion of Henry James no illustration to a book of his should have any direct bearing upon it. He believed that the prose itself should be good enough, interesting enough and, 'if the question be of picture, pictorial enough, above all *in itself...*'

Umberto Eco wrote that the title of a book 'must muddle the reader's ideas, not regiment them.'

In my opinion, language and meaning are muddled enough without trying to accentuate the difficulties.

Something about the spirit of a book 'suits' a particular title; and author, publisher and designer should strive for a consonance between text, title and cover (even though the author may not be the best judge of what is appropriate). Despite the dogmas of Misters James and Eco, I hope that between Jo O'Donoghue, my editor, Claire McVeigh, the cover designer, and myself, that that objective has been achieved.

When people asked me what I was currently writing, I would reply, 'A book of essays.'

'Ooom. I see,' they would say, before turning to the question of the weather.

'Essays?' said Joe O'Connor, a fellow author. 'You want it to sell, don't you? Call it anything but a book of essays!'

What was I writing? Some pieces. Politics and Literature. A memoir.

For a title I liked the idea of *Down To Grovetree,* as a tribute to the staff of my mother's residential home. Then, at another stage in this work, it struck me that many of the pieces I had been writing were about dead people – relatives, friends, comrades, informers, soldiers, writers and composers. And when I look in my notebooks I see I have gathered a preponderance of quotations on the subject of old age and mortality from writers, poets and philosophers.

I then thought to call the book *The Dead*, but that title, though a legitimate choice, might have suggested an attempt to capitalise on James Joyce.

On a miserable wet afternoon in March, I was showing two literary friends, Tina Neylon from Cork and Seamus Hosey from County Laois, around Milltown Cemetery and was telling them about the difficulties I was having in naming my book. Seamus stopped and said: 'What about that line from *Godot* – "All the dead voices"?' He declaimed the exchanges between Estragon and Vladimir from Beckett's *Waiting For Godot*.

I had another stab at reading the play soon after.

Estragon: All the dead voices.
Vladimir: They make a noise like wings.
Estragon: Like leaves.
Vladimir: Like sand.
Estragon: Like leaves.

[*Silence*]

Vladimir: They all speak at once.
Estragon: Each one to itself.

[*Silence*]

Vladimir: Rather they whisper.
Estragon: They rustle.
Vladimir: They murmur.
Estragon: They rustle.

[*Silence*]

Vladimir: What do they say?

Estragon: They talk about their lives.

Vladimir: To have lived is not enough for them.

Estragon: They have to talk about it.

Vladimir: To be dead is not enough for them.

Estragon: It is not sufficient.

[Silence]

Vladimir: They make a noise like feathers.

Estragon: Like leaves.

Vladimir: Like ashes.

Estragon: Like leaves.

[Long silence]

I found myself being captivated by the power of the play and how Beckett dramatises our entrapment, our inability to control our lives, our suffering, the anomie the individual experiences within society, and our sense of angst, ennui and desperation, which should, logically, compel us to suicide.

Instead, we human beings are prepared to wait (as if it were a choice), hoping that life might improve the next day – or might even begin to improve – even though tomorrow we are one day closer to death and the dead.

For me, the real strength of the play is that despite whatever unknowable, unseen force plagues them, despite the fact that Vladimir and Estragon admit to being happier when apart, they address each other with terms of endearment – Didi and Gogo – and there is between them the solidarity of love: 'Come here till I embrace you'; 'Stay with me!' 'Did I ever leave you?'; 'There, there . . . Didi is there . . . don't be afraid . . . '

Don't be afraid.

Don't be afraid – of life, of death.

Of all the dead voices.

Some of these writings first appeared as short subjects in my weekly column in the *Andersonstown News*, in the *Irish Examiner*, or other newspapers, though here I have tried to arrange and meld them felicitously with the new pieces in a roughly chronological order that reflects something of the times in my life, the people I met and observed, or learnt about, and thought about afterwards.

The one piece which is a 'pastiche' of fact and fiction is 'The Lakes', which is based on an amalgam of real events in the lives of several people I knew, though the names have been changed. There is also a little bit of cheating – or an example of poetic licence – when at the end of 'Old Friends' I conflate two extracts from Wordsworth's *The Prelude*: the first part-stanza is from Book Second, 'School-time' (continued), the second is from Book Fifth.

I am also glad to say that my old friend Billy, the subject of that piece, not only had a wonderful ninetieth birthday at his home, which was full of friends and neighbours, but a few months later became a great-great-grandfather. He was still partying at four in the morning. There was one major disappointment, he said afterwards. Throughout the night he was hoping that his daughter Rita would walk through the door for the first time since 1971. Rita O'Hare is Sinn Féin's representative in Washington, who, four years after the signing of the Good Friday Agreement, is still banned by the British government from coming home and faces prosecution over a shooting incident thirty-one years ago, involving the British army and the IRA, in which she was wounded.

I said to Billy that we should immediately begin planning his ninety-first birthday party. He eloquently recited the first few lines from Walter De La Mare's poem, 'Farewell':

> When I lie where shades of darkness
> Shall no more assail mine eyes,
> Nor the rain make lamentation
> When the wind sighs:

How will fare the world whose wonder
Was the very proof of me?

Then he said, 'Do you think I'll still be around?' and smiled.
'You'll still be here and we'll still be drinking,' I said, and told
him about the interview I had read a few years ago with the
oldest man in the world, a 119-year-old Japanese fisherman.
His longevity was ascribed to his diet of oily fish, rice wine
and a spartan lifestyle.

He was interviewed in his home, a hut, by a female
journalist, and at one stage he got into bed, which consisted
of a board and a bit of straw, covered by a blanket. The young
journalist was surprised when he rolled a cigarette and began
smoking. Was he not concerned about damaging his health,
she asked, and he looked at her, as if to say there were few
enough pleasures in this life.

She asked him how long he had been smoking and he said
he took it up when the wife died.

'What age were you then?' she asked.

Going on ninety-nine, he replied. He leaned back and
produced a bottle of sake from the corner of the bed, which
he opened, and asked, would she like a drink, as he was going
to have some. She declined.

'Are you sure?' he asked again, smiling.

And she wrote that when he asked her the second time
she recognised in the sparkle of his eyes the warmth, drive
and familiar flicker of desire, the wonderful gift of life.

Edmund Burkes
Irish Identicles
See or I. Donec
J.A.P.